IREDI WAR
a folkscript

DRAMA

Kraftgriots

Also in the series (DRAMA)

IREDI WAR
a folkscript
DRAMA

Sam Ukala

kraftgriots

Published by

Kraft Books Limited
6A Polytechnic Road, Sango, Ibadan
Box 22084, University of Ibadan Post Office
Ibadan, Oyo State, Nigeria
☎ +234(0)803 348 2474, +234(0)805 129 1191
E-mail: kraftbooks@yahoo.com
www.kraftbookslimited.com

First published 2014

ISBN 978–978–918–159–9

= KRAFTGRIOTS =
(A literary imprint of Kraft Books Limited)

First printing, February 2014
Second printing, January 2015

Dedication

To the memory of
Warriors of Ekumeku
And Iredi Wars
and to
Their descendants
In spirit and in truth

Preface

Iredi War is based on the history of the 1906 uprising of the people of Owa Kingdom, currently in Ika North-East Local Government Area of Delta State of Nigeria, against British oppressive colonial rule, as championed by Assistant District Commissioner O.S. Crewe-Read (whom the Owa called Iredi), and the quelling of it by the British Army. Historical accounts of this are presented in two publications: "The Murder of OS Crewe-Read, the Attack on EC Crewe-Read and the Political Officers AA Chichester & AC Douglas who Directed the Reprisals against the Insurgents" by Keith Steward FRGS and Chief Dan A. Agbobu's "The Historical Evolution of Owa Kingdom" in K.O. Echenim, ed. *Ndiowa and their Monarchs: An Overview*. Though the first is much more detailed, the bone structures of the two accounts are essentially the same, and both of them portray the indiscretion and high-handedness of OS Crewe-Read and the brutality of the reprisal attack.

Iredi War is a "folkist" play or a "folkscript" because it is constructed by the principles of "Folkism", which I define as

> the tendency to base literary plays on the history, culture, and concerns of the folk (the 'people in general'...), and to compose and perform them in accordance with African conventions for composing and performing the folktale".
> ("'Folkism': Towards a National Aesthetic Principle for Nigerian Dramaturgy". *New Theatre Quarterly* XII (47), Aug. 1996: 279-287.)

In Folkism, the dramatic recreation or adaptation of a story is faithful to the original, not slavishly, but enough for the owners of the story to recognize it and identify with the recreation or adaptation; the plot is simple; language is familiar but imagistic; the story is run-on like the folktale, not structured in Acts and Scenes, and with no stoppages for scene-changing; staging is, therefore, simultaneous; the performance structure allows for robust audience participation and extempore response of the narrator and performers to relevant unscripted lines from the public audience, sometimes formally represented by the MOA (Member(s) of the Audience). Finally, in Folkism, moral instruction comes with entertainment.

I wish to acknowledge Keith Steward FRGS and Chief Dan A. Agbobu and the Owa Stakeholders Forum for their aforementioned publications on this crucial aspect of the history of Owa. I am thankful to Professor Kester Echenim for calling my attention to Keith Steward's work and for reading the manuscript of *Iredi War* and offering useful advice. Hon. Justice (Chief) S.A. Ehiwario also read the manuscript and made useful suggestions, for which I am deeply indebted to him. I cannot sufficiently thank the Obi of Owa, Dr E.O. Efeizomor, for his friendship, encouragement and support in many ways. Finally, I ascribe all the glory and honour to Almighty God for the inspiration, energy and resources vested in this work, which, hopefully, would be of use to all those who believe that history – even with all its setbacks – is the cornerstone for building an enviable future.

Sam Ukala
January 2014

Characters

NARRATOR I
(Also JAMBA)   –   Court Messenger/Runner

NARRATOR II
(Also AFOPELE)   –   Senior Court Messenger/Runner

IGBOBA or HEAD
CHIEF EKTUI   –   The Obi of Owa Kingdom

NNEKA   –   Wife of Igboba

NWOMA   –   Another wife of Igboba

NWOBI   –   Prince and brother of Igboba

ACHOLEM   –   The Iyase (Prime Minister), a palace chief

IWEKUBA   –   The Odogwu (War Minister), a palace chief

EKOME   –   Another palace chief

DIBIE   –   Priest and diviner

ONYELA   –   Youth Leader I

UZUN   –   Assistant Youth Leader

EBIE   –   Youth Leader II, son of Iwekuba

YOUTHS/WARRIORS

GUARDS OF THE PALACE/ATTENDANTS

CREWE-READ   –   Assistant District Commissioner (ADC), Agbor Sub-District

LAWANI   –   Police Sergeant

POLICE CONSTABLES (Six in Number)

GILPIN   –   Court Clerk

OMOZEFI   –   Court Messenger/Runner

CHICHESTER, District Commissioner (DC), Agbor, Acting Provincial Commissioner (APC)

CAPT. RUDKIN   –   Commander, Area Command, West African Frontier Force (WAFF), Asaba

DR BATE
SOLDIERS
CARRIERS/RUNNERS
STRANGERS
M.O.A., MEMBER(S) OF THE AUDIENCE, players seated in the
audience. Also TOWNSPEOPLE
AUDIENCE   –   The public audience
MUSICIANS/PERFORMERS/MAIDENS/VOICES

The play is set in Owa in what is now known as Ika North-East Local Government Area; Agbor, in Ika South Local Government Area; and Asaba, in Oshimili South Local Government Area, all in Delta State of Nigeria. Time is June to August, 1906.

The Beginning

Three-quarter arena formation. Half of the arena is the performance area while the other half is the audience area. The performance area has four parts: stage centre is the Owa palace court; stage right is the Office of Army Area Command, Asaba, which later becomes the Office of the District Commissioner at Agbor; stage left is Owa forest with a tent that would house the camp of O.S. CREWE-READ, the Assistant District Commissioner (ADC); the broad frontage of these settings (or a broad apron if a proscenium stage is adapted), represents the townsquare and later the road to and fro Owa-Nta. Though time of story is mid-1906, the time of telling is today. The changes in the locales may be indicated by signposts or posters, though they are also communicated in the dialogue.

Moonlight. Many TOWNSPEOPLE, M.O.A., and members of the public AUDIENCE, are already gathered (or seated) while some more are hurrying in. PERFORMERS in costumes have also gathered at the townsquare, some sitting, some standing in corners, rehearsing their lines or playing some musical instruments in low tones. Spotlight on NARRATOR I among the AUDIENCE.

NARRATOR I: (*Rises, and with her right hand, casts imaginary white chalk powder at the* AUDIENCE.) *E ye m onu nzun!* (I give you white chalk!)

AUDIENCE: *I gwo, o re-e!* (If you concoct, may it be efficacious!)

(*The above arousal call and response is done thrice as* NARRATOR I *approaches the performance area. Once there, she raises a song.*)

Luni ilu	Tell a tale
Ilu I-gboba	Tale of I-gboba
Do n'udo	Tug at the rope
Udo Kpirikpiri	It's unsnappable

11

Some performers soon accompany the singing with drums and other instruments while others dance. This infects the AUDIENCE *many of whom now join in singing, clapping or dancing till* NARRATOR II, *spotlighted in the audience chin-in-hand, hurtles forward and stops the music.*)

NARRATOR II: Thank you! Thank you! But, please, sit down. (*To* NARRATOR I.) You shouldn't have turned that song into a dance.

NARRATOR I: Why?

NARRATOR II: Tonight's tale is not a happy tale.

NARRATOR I: A tale is a tale, my brother. Now that the people have sung and danced, they have been activated in their minds and bodies to get the best out of our story. (*To* AUDIENCE.) Or haven't you?

AUDIENCE: We have!

NARRATOR II: Okay. (*To* AUDIENCE.) People, we have this proverb: "One does not sit in his own home and crush his scrotum in the process". But our story tonight belies that proverb.

NARRATOR I: Yes. Obi Igboba of Owa was sitting in his palace and he crushed his ... Say it, if you dare.

NARRATOR II: That's why I said it's a sad tale.

NARRATOR I: But there's also hope in the song we danced to. They tugged at Igboba, the rope, but he couldn't be snapped.

NARRATOR II: Yes, my sister. But if they made *you* crush your scrotum, would you say you haven't snapped?

NARRATOR I: (*Checks herself for a scrotum.*) Well, I don't have a scrotum.

NARRATOR II: I have, and I can tell you that it's a tragedy to crush it. But, sometimes, you sit in your own home and crush your scrotum!

NARRATOR I: But we must tell this story, whether it makes us cry or not. And ... (*Gestures at* PERFORMERS.) ... no one here can tell it better than us.

(*With loud hisses and shaking of their heads,* PERFORMERS *exit in different directions.*)

M.O.A.: See! They're angry!

NARRATOR I: No ... they cannot be. They are in us. We merely displayed them for you to know them.

NARRATOR II: We tell parts of the story—

NARRATOR I: —and enact parts. And when we enact—

NARRATOR II: —we summon them from our bowel—

NARRATOR I: —our mind,

NARRATOR II: —our head.

NARRATOR I: We externalise them as demonstrations—

NARRATOR II: —as illustrations in the book of our story—

NARRATOR I & NARRATOR II: —for your better understanding!

NARRATOR I: Can you guess another reason why even they can't tell the story better than the two of us?

AUDIENCE: Tell us!

NARRATOR II: Our grandfathers were part of it. Mine was a carrier and a runner. He carried the whiteman's loads. He even carried the white man himself, if the journey was long and the terrain tough. He also ran swiftly across long distances—

NARRATOR I: —like a white man's dog!

NARRATOR II: (*Feigning anger.*) Your father! ... My grandfather ran across long distances to deliver telegrams from town to town. Runners were the mobile phones of those days, not dogs! (*Looks at* NARRATOR I.)

NARRATOR I: (*Thumbing her chest.*) My own grandfather was a soldier in the West African Frontier Force (WAFF). From Benin to Calabar, anywhere any native community raised its ugly head of protest against whatever the white man wanted, my grandfather and others like him were quickly drafted there to pour fire on that community!

NARRATOR II: Like mindless slaves, killing one another to please their master!

NARRATOR I: (*Feigning anger.*) Your father! ... (*To* AUDIENCE.) My people, it was within that dark period of our history that there was June, 1906. There was the kingdom of Owa. There was Igboba, the Obi of Owa.

NARRATOR II: And there was Crewe-Read, Offley Stuart Crewe-Read, the Assistant District Commissioner (ADC), Agbor Sub-District. Owa people called him, "Iredi" or "Ikuru-Iredi".

(*Lights on the Owa palace court, decorated with paintings and carvings hanging on the wall. A low shrine is prominent at the left corner of its entrance. IGBOBA, 99, in full royal regalia, is on the throne. An attendant is standing behind his right arm, carrying the ada (scimitar); another is standing to the left, gently fanning him with an animal-skin fan. Seated before him, on a bench to the right, are his chiefs - ACHOLEM, 87, IWEKUBA, 75, and EKOME, 50. NWOBI, 65, Igboba's brother, is sitting on a separate chair. A few TOWNSPEOPLE, including ONYELA, the Youth Leader, are standing behind the chiefs. Seated to the left of the throne are CREWE-READ, a white man about 25 years of age, wearing a helmet, LAWANI, 45, in police sergeant's uniform, and GILPIN, 50, carrying a file with sheets of paper, upon which he occasionally scribbles. An armed, stern-looking African police CONSTABLE stands behind CREWE-READ, while three other CONSTABLES stand about on guard. On the floor between the chiefs and CREWE-READ are a heap of yams, some bunches of plantain, a tin of palm oil and a keg of frothy palm wine.* UZUN *has just served kola and many are chewing theirs. He drops the bowl with the remaining kola nuts on a stool before* CREWE-READ. *He takes up the keg of palm wine, shakes it gently, and serves* IGBOBA.)

IGBOBA: (*Pouring libation.*) Gods of our land! Wine has come. Our ancestors—

CREWE-READ: (*To* IGBOBA.) Excuse me, Chief Igboba (*Pronounced by him as "Aig-bo-ba".*) Perhaps, you haven't noticed that I didn't chew your kola. (*Raises and drops on the table the lobe that he was served.*)

IGBOBA: You didn't chew it? Why, Mr ADC?

CREWE-READ: DC will do. (*As* IGBOBA *makes to speak again.*) Don't rigmarole, Chief Igboba. I said, DC will do.

IGBOBA: OK, Mr DC. Why didn't you chew your—?

CREWE-READ: Because you first offered it to your jujus—

IGBOBA: Our gods and anc—

CREWE-READ: Jujus! That's what they are! On my first visit, I rejected your kola and palm wine for the same reason. Perhaps, you were too insensitive to notice ... For Christ's sake, can't you pray to God Almighty, the Alpha and Omega, the Omnipresent, Omnipotent, Omniscient?

EKOME: Hmm! Omini-mini! (*Laughter from* IGBOBA *and* TOWNSPEOPLE.)

CREWE-READ: What's funny?

IGBOBA: (*Still laughing.*) The names of your god, Mr ADC.

CREWE-READ: (*Severely.*) DC!

IGBOBA: OK, DC ... My people have just heard the names of your god for the first time and they find them funny.

EKOME: Especially the omini-mini-mini!

15

IGBOBA: So, you see, Mr DC, we *do not* know your god. Our fathers didn't introduce him to us. That's why we don't offer him kola and palm wine.

CREWE-READ: Chief Igboba, your fathers were primitive, ignorant and uncivilized barbarians.

IGBOBA: We still are. Haven't you said that to us in many ways? How can we now make white the black nose of the dog?

CREWE-READ: Which dog? Who's talking about—? (GILPIN *whispers to him.*) Of course, I understand. This indolent and wobbly rigmarole with words is a sure index of their primitiveness ... Now, Chief Igboba, to make white the black nose of the dog, that was why I sent those preachers to you, those evangelists, your fellow Blacks, who have seen the light. But how did you receive them?

IGBOBA: Very well, Mr DC. It's a pity they came once and haven't returned. Perhaps, they're still searching for an answer to the question I asked them.

CREWE-READ: Which was?

IGBOBA: If a stranger entered your house, would your children adopt him as their father and throw you out of the house?

(*Free comments from the chiefs and* TOWNSPEOPLE *in appreciation of Igboba's wisdom.*)

CREWE-READ: (*After a grin.*) That was a knockout, wasn't it? But mark my word: tomorrow at noon, you'll get your answer. Tomorrow at noon. Arrangement for that has since been completed.

IGBOBA: *Arrangement* for my answer?

CREWE-READ: Oh, yes.

IGBOBA: (*Pouts and nods a few times before speaking.*) Onyela!

ONYELA: *(Bows deeply.)* Obi Agun!

IGBOBA: Serve the white man as he wants.

ONYELA: Yes, my lord.

(From in front of his feet, apparently hidden behind the chiefs, ONYELA picks up a keg of palm wine and a bowl of kola nuts, which he places on the stool before CREWE-READ.)

IGBOBA: Let tomorrow come, Mr DC, and Igboba will be here to receive your answer. We hope it'd be a straight and direct answer, not an indolent, wobbly rigmarole like ours ... Your gifts are before you and you may now offer them to your god.

EKOME: Your omini-mini-mini!

IWEKUBA: But where is our friendship with the white man if we can't share kola and palm wine with him?

IGBOBA: *(Ignoring IWEKUBA's question.)* Our gods and ancestors! Wine has come. *(Pours some wine on the floor.)* Drink and bless us.

TOWNSPEOPLE: Iseh!

IGBOBA: May our eyes not see what eyes have never seen.

TOWNSPEOPLE: Iseh!

(As IGBOBA continues with pouring libation, CREWE-READ and his men stand and stretch their hands towards their gifts as GILPIN prays bombastically while his party choruses a loud "Amen" at appropriate intervals. This goes on simultaneously with Igboba's prayer, to which his party choruses a loud "Iseh" at appropriate intervals. Each party apparently strives to outdo the other. At the end of the prayers, IGBOBA hands the cup to NWOBI, who drinks on his behalf, after which ONYELA and UZUN serve the chiefs and TOWNSPEOPLE. Simultaneously, GILPIN breaks the visitors' kola nuts and a constable serves everyone in their

party, beginning with CREWE-READ. *Then he serves palm wine to only* CREWE-READ *and* GILPIN.)

CREWE-READ: (*Sips the palm wine, nods, gulps it, then drops his cup on the table.*) Good! Now to the business of the day, Chief Igboba. I need more carriers.

IGBOBA: More carriers!

CREWE-READ: Yes, more carriers. Able-bodied, vivacious young men.

IGBOBA: We gave you *fifty* last time!

CREWE-READ: And I want fifty more.

ACHOLEM: (*Rising to his feet.*) Obi Agun! Reign forever! May I remind us of something? On that occasion, we agreed that those fifty would be returned to us alive before we send another batch, if necessary.

NWOBI: *Gbam*! Exactly what we said.

IGBOBA: Mr DC, Tortoise said—

CREWE-READ: Can you imagine! He even converses with the tortoise!

IGBOBA: (*Amused.*) Oh, yes, we do. When Tortoise was asked to visit the lion, who was ill, he said, "I saw the footmarks that went into the lion's den, but didn't see any that came out of it. Until I see footmarks returning from the lion's den, I'm not—

IGBOBA/TOWNSPEOPLE: —going there"!

IWEKUBA: Besides, this is farming season in a farming community. We need able-bodied young men to produce the yams, palm oil and palm wine that you carry away each time you visit.

CREWE-READ: Chief Igboba! Call your chiefs to order or I'll have them flogged.

(*Expressions of shock from* TOWNSPEOPLE. *At once*

18

LAWANI *and a constable, each with a horsewhip, rise and deploy themselves to observe* TOWNSPEOPLE.)

Only you may address me. You can see that my people are quiet while I talk. That's the mark of civilisation.

IGBOBA: These are palace chiefs, Mr DC. You cannot flog them.

CREWE-READ: Don't dare me.

IGBOBA: Well, those of you carrying canes, listen very carefully. Any hand that flogs any chief here shall swell up to the neck of its owner and strangle him. Don't say you were not warned.

CREWE-READ: Nonsense! Mere superstition!

IGBOBA: Let them try ... You see, Mr DC., you cannot shut my chiefs up because I value their views on issues. And, in our culture, the Obi owns the land and the land—

IGBOBA/TOWNSPEOPLE: —owns the Obi.

CREWE-READ: I'm *not* concerned about your culture, which is uncivilised, anyway. I'm concerned about protocol in the Southern Protectorate under His Majesty King Edward VII, King of the United Kingdom and the British Dominions, in whose service I am.

ACHOLEM: (*Rising again.*) Obi Agun! Reign forever! May I remind us—

CREWE-READ: Chief Igboba! Call your chief to order—

IWEKUBA: (*Impatiently.*) White man! He's addressing his own king, not you or your king!

CREWE-READ: My king is king here also! Don't you ever forget that. Owa is nothing but a teeny-weeny part of the British Dominions.

IWEKUBA: Meaning there's no King of Owa anymore?

CREWE-READ: I've never addressed him as a king, have I?

19

NWOBI: No, you haven't. (*To* IWEKUBA.) Indeed, he has never. And it's all getting clearer now ... (*To* IGBOBA.) My brother, what the white man is saying is that you should come down from the throne, the throne of your fathers, because (*Pointing at* CREWE-READ.) he does not recognize you as the king of Owa! Because the throne you sit on now belongs to one Eduwardu, whose bottom spreads like the clouds over a thousand thrones, thrones of both Oyibo and African ancestors! Ikuru-Iredi says Obi Agun should climb down the throne!

IWEKUBA: It's his own king that will climb down. Ikuru-Iredi! What's he kuru-ing?

EKOME: May we not sit in our own home and, in sitting, crush our scrotum.

TOWNSPEOPLE: Iseh!

NWOBI: But what scrotum do we have left? We are talking about his not calling him "King"; he doesn't even call him "Head Chief", which the real DC, Chichester, calls him. This *small boy* simply calls our king "Chief". He levels him up with every other chief! And you still think we have a scrotum?

(TOWNSPEOPLE *get tumultuous.* LAWANI *and the constable attempt to quieten them by raising their whips at them, but they remain unruly until* IGBOBA *raises his right hand at them with his palm open.*)

IGBOBA: My people, please, be patient. Let's hear DC out. I am the snake on the palm tree. I won't attack the palm-tree climber at sight because I can't tell immediately whether he's going about his own business or coming after me.

ACHOLEM: Obi Agun! May I remind us that what the white man said just now is much more than coming after the snake. It has already cudgelled the snake on the head.

EKOME: God forbid!

20

CREWE-READ: For the last time, Chief Igboba, call your chiefs to order!

IWEKUBA: And what would you do, if he doesn't?

GILPIN: (*To* IWEKUBA.) Mr man, you need to maintain demonstrable decorum and tangible tranquillity.

IWEKUBA: (*Moving towards* GILPIN.) Go tell your father that, do you hear? I said, Go—

IGBOBA: Iwe-ku-baaa!

IWEKUBA: Obi Agun! You heard this whiteman's dog curse me, didn't you?

GILPIN: I didn't curse you, Chief.

IGBOBA: Odogwu! Go back to your seat, please. (IWEKUBA *obeys*.) Go on, Mr DC. We're listening.

CREWE-READ: As I was saying before I was interrupted in an—

CREWE-READ/IGBOBA: —uncivilised manner—

CREWE-READ: —I need more carriers. The Empire is expanding. And, as you can see, Blacks everywhere are difficult to govern because they are primitive, excessively emotional and unreasoning. They cause a lot of trouble, which causes us to frequently move administrators, officers, men and materials from district to district, town to town. And, of course, one must give this to them: Blacks are also very hospitable. Everywhere we go, you present us with gifts like these ... (*Points to the gifts on the floor.*) ... and we need carriers to move them to our base.

IGBOBA: Is that all?

CREWE-READ: Not exactly. I also require every adult citizen of Owa to pay a levy of two shillings only.

(TOWNSPEOPLE *protest again until* IGBOBA *raises his open palm.*)

IGBOBA: Is that all, Mr DC?

CREWE-READ: Well, for now, yes.

IGBOBA: You've spoken well, Mr DC.

IWEKUBA: So well indeed! At least, he didn't ask for our testicles.

ACHOLEM: Or our wives.

(ACHOLEM *signs to the chiefs. They put their heads together and confer in a whisper.* CONSTABLE *serves* CREWE-READ *more palm wine.*)

IGBOBA: (*As* ADC *drinks.*) Mr DC, our people say that it's where it pains one that one shows to the doctor. You've showed us where it pains you.

CREWE-READ: I've no pains whatsoever and you can't be my doctor. (*Drinks.*)

IGBOBA: I know ... But there's an aspect of your pain that we can treat at once.

CREWE-READ: I said I've no—

IGBOBA: We'll ask some young men to take your gifts to Agbor for you and come back. (CREWE-READ *makes to speak, but* IGBOBA *continues.*) I hope your palm wine is good.

CREWE-READ: Very good.

IGBOBA: Do have some more while my chiefs confer and advise me on the other aspects of your pain.

ACHOLEM: (*Standing.*) Obi Agun! Long may you live! Your chiefs have conferred already. They've asked me to tell you that the demands of Mr Ikuru-Iredi are too weighty for the few of us here to dispose of, negatively or positively. They are also too heavy for our lips to convey to the people of Owa, knowing that they recently gave the white man *fifty* hefty carriers and have been paying levies of yams and palm oil to the white man, periodically, supposedly for the upkeep of road menders. Your Majesty, your chiefs say, let the white man use his own mouth to tell the people of Owa what he wants since he has refused to take our NO as the NO of our people. (*To the chiefs.*) Did I speak your mind?

CHIEFS: Yes!

IGBOBA: Thank you, my chiefs ... You heard them, Mr DC. That's what we say.

CREWE-READ: Brilliant! Who's afraid of addressing the people of Owa directly? Indeed, your chiefs apparently read my mind. I can't afford to have my urgent instructions passed to the people through an indolent and wobbly rigmarole with words. 5 pm tomorrow then.

IGBOBA: You had said 12 noon.

CREWE-READ: 12 noon is for the answer to your puzzle. That answer should put you in the right frame of mind for the meeting at 5 pm. Townsquare. Gather all able-bodied men and women. I'll personally pick those who'd be suitable for the honour of carrierhood in His Majesty's Service. And - this is important - instruct every adult to come with their levies. Two shillings.

(*He rises. All rise, except* IGBOBA *and* IWEKUBA. ONYELA *and* UZUN *begin to organise young townspeople to move the gifts off the ground. Fade out.*)

Crackling noise of fire. Spotlights on NARRATOR II *on the right side of the townsquare. The hymn, "Onward Christian Soldiers" wells up in the distance and remains in the background.*

NARRATOR II: Fire! Fire!! My people, fire on every shrine! The Christian Soldiers, the missionaries, they came to Owa with the Bible in the left hand and fire in the right. They wetted every god, every ancestor, with kerosene; they wetted their shrines, and set them all ablaze!

(Spotlight on NARRATOR I *on the left side of the townsquare.)*

NARRATOR I: That was the answer that came at 12 noon! Like Elijah's prayer, Igboba's puzzle was answered by fire! Igboba was promptly seated in his court at 12 noon, waiting for Mr DC to come with an answer, not knowing that the answer was already ravaging the length and breath of Owa. The father of the house, the father of the house, was not sent out of his house because of the stranger; instead, he was burnt along with his house! The people's gods and ancestors were desecrated and burnt to ashes! Oh, Owa!

MOA I: Who were those missionaries?

NARRATOR II: *(Spotlighted again.)* Our black brothers, who, according to the DC, had "seen the light"! Our own kith and kin. They spat and farted on our gods and ancestors, and set them ablaze. Only a white man was with them, *one* white man, silently masterminding twenty Blacks.

MOA II: Why didn't Owa attack them?

NARRATOR II: Onyela, the Youth Leader, will soon tell us.

(The Christian soldiers' song swells up again, but a traditional dirge soon fades in to drown it. Slowly, lights come on Igboba's court. IGBOBA is alone, ruminating and slowly pacing the floor. In his right hand is a white horse-

tail whisk. The dirge softens but remains in the background.)

IGBOBA: (*Now at the shrine.*) My gods and ancestors, each time I gave you kola to eat or palm wine to drink I prayed you not to let me see what eyes have never seen. Now, what is this I'm seeing? Which Obi before me saw this? You're spirits, I know. You couldn't be confined in a shrine. Therefore, you couldn't have been burnt by the (*Enter ACHOLEM and IWEKUBA, unnoticed.*) whiteman's fire. But (*Takes up a carving of an ancestor from the shrine.*) ... wood carvings like this symbolize you. They are your concrete presence among us. Those burnt carvings made you the physical and visible fathers of our houses, who watched over us. Those burnt shrines were your houses in our family compounds. Why couldn't you defend them? Why? (*Makes to kneel.*)

ACHOLEM, IWEKUBA: Obi Agun!

(IGBOBA *does not respond, but slowly drops the carving and turns to his visitors.* NWOBI *and* EKOME *also rush in and pay him homage. Again, he does not respond.*)

IGBOBA: Why do you all greet me like a king?

ACHOLEM: Why does Your Majesty ask such a—

IGBOBA: What's happening to me, did it ever happen to any of my predecessors? The goat has eaten up the palm fronds on my head and you still call me "Obi, the Lion"! (*Sternly to* EKOME.) Will the goat dare to eat the palm fronds on a lion's head? I ask you!

EKOME: No, my Lord. (IGBOBA *strides to the throne and sits, visibly troubled.*)

ACHOLEM: Don't be unfair to yourself, my lord. It's not your fault. May I remind us of our neighbours – the Binis and the Itsekiris. Only a few years ago, what's happening to Owa happened to their kingdoms.

NWOBI: Obi Agun! They'd soon be here – the youth leaders.

IGBOBA: Thank you, my brother. The town crier, have you also instructed him?

NWOBI: Yes, Your Majesty.

IWEKUBA: Town Crier! To do what, My Lord?

IGBOBA: The message was for the town crier, Iwekuba. You'll hear him when he cries. (*To* ACHOLEM.) Iyase, it's not my fault?

ACHOLEM: No, My Lord.

IGBOBA: Mm-hmm ... Not the fault of Ovonramwen of Bini?

ACHOLEM: No, My Lord.

IGBOBA: Not the fault of Nana of Itsekiri land?

ACHOLEM: No, My Lord.

MOA I: Whose fault was it then?

MOA II: That of the white man?

IWEKUBA: Ask him, my brother. He's been arguing with me. Iyase, if a stranger climbed your wife on your own bed in your presence and you did nothing, whose fault would it be? The stranger's or your wife's? ... It's our fault, Iyase. We shouldn't leave the face of a word and speak its back.

NWOBI: How's it our fault, Odogwu? We were here waiting peacefully for a peaceful answer to a peaceful question and—

IWEKUBA: I didn't mean the palace. At least, the palace shrine is still intact. The traitors didn't dare come here to set it ablaze. I meant *us*, those of us who saw the abomination as it was being committed all over Owa and did nothing. We are to blame.

ACHOLEM: I disagree. If a stranger climbs your wife on your own bed in your presence, your question should be, why did the stranger enter your own house and not your neighbour's? Why did your god not blind his eye to your house and to your wife? Your ancestors standing on guard at the entrance to your compound (*Pointing at the shrine.*) ... like those ones over there, why didn't they divert the steps of the evil stranger? You just noted that the shrine here is still intact. Why did the burners-of-shrines not see it? Did anyone have to fight to defend it?

EKOME: I agree with you, Iyase. The gods and ancestors of the Bini and the Itsekiri were, probably, drunk and asleep. Drunk with too much blood and wine of sacrifice! Our gods and ancestors might have been drunk too.

IGBOBA: Don't talk anyhow about our gods and ancestors!

EKOME: I'm sorry, Your Majesty. But I'm speaking the face of the word and not its back. How could our gods and ancestors let this happen in the reign of one who has never denied them whatever was their due? How could they have tucked their tails in-between their thighs at the sight of mere servants of Omini-mini?

IWEKUBA: Ekobi, you're speaking the back of the word by blaming our gods for our cowardice. Assuming our gods were drunk and asleep, if your father was drunk and asleep, would you let an evil stranger set him and his house ablaze?

EKOME: I'm not a warrior like you, my elder. My father was not a warrior. Maybe, because you are War Minister, you think we should fight all wars, including the ones our gods ought to fight for us or for themselves. But all I'm saying is that we sacrifice to our gods and ancestors and, in return, they should protect us. If it's now our duty to protect them, then they should first come and sacrifice to us.

IGBOBA: You are young, Ekome, and speak like a child. You just told us that it was the servants of Omini-mini that set our shrines ablaze. Or was it Omini-mini himself?

EKOME: No, Your Majesty.

27

(*Enter* ONYELA *and* UZUN. *They pay homage to* IGBOBA, *but he does not respond.*)

IWEKUBA: Your Majesty, I saw them with my two naked eyes. There was no god among them. It's so painful to me that they fought for their god and our young men, led by these two (*Points to* ONYELA *and* UZUN.) ... couldn't fight for our gods and ancestors. I watched those vandals and cursed my age. You all know what I could have done when I was the youth leader.

EKOME: What has age to do with it? If I were the War Minister, truly eager to fight for my gods, I wouldn't have considered my age. I would have single-handedly quaked those vandals to death. Or, at least, I would have had Owa say of me: this is where Ekome died, fighting gallantly, than this is where Ekome stood, like a woman, watching the uncircumcised rape our land.

IWEKUBA: (*Who has been looking at* EKOME *with a pout, bursts into laughter.*) Don't make me laugh, Ekome. A few moments ago, you confessed that your father was not a warrior and you're not. But I can tell you that it goes further back. Your grandfather, your great grandfather, your great great grandfather, your great, great, great grand—

EKOME: Did you know them?

IWEKUBA: Yes, of course. Knowing you is knowing them. They were all cowards, and you took after them. So, don't just fill your belly with palm wine and wish you were War Minister! The mere news of war, coming, will kill you with diarrhoea, *utoro!*

(*Laughter.*)

ONYELA: It's my fault, Chief Ekome, not the fault of the War Minister. He has since retired from active service and we don't expect him to continue to lead Owa in battle. That's my duty now. And I'm sorry I failed Owa this time.

(*Moves towards the throne and kneels, followed by* UZUN.)
Forgive me, Your Majesty.

UZUN: Forgive us, My Lord.

ONYELA: The strangers took us unawares. It certainly took some days for them to mobilise for action. But, if it was just one of them that came to attack Owa and I saw him, I'd have single-handedly fed him with his own flesh. But, if anyone had single handedly attacked all those people who came with fire and guns, it'd have been like a foolish cockroach attacking a pack of hungry cocks. We needed to mobilise our youths, and, as you know, we stay scattered all over the eight settlements of Owa. Besides, the attack was at noon while we were all engaged in the farms. The deed was done before a significant number of our people arrived at the scene. Please, bear with us.

IGBOBA: Rise, loyal ones, rise. The fart that would disgrace a man doesn't come through the middle of his anus; it escapes through the side. Rise. (*They rise.*) Like a treacherous snake, the white man has struck us and slid off. We won't let him take us unawares again, would we?

ONYELA, UZUN: No, My Lord!

IGBOBA: That means you have mobilised everyone now?

ONYELA: To a large extent, Your Majesty! We are still mobilising.

IGBOBA: Be fast about it.

IWEKUBA: Water yam is eaten in haste.

IGBOBA: Yes. If the old one stays too long at the latrine, vultures mistake him for a carcass. Henceforth, we must all stand like the ears of the hound. If we do sleep at all, we must sleep like the cat. You may go.

ONYELA: Obi Agun! If I may say this, there's one other

reason why we wouldn't have attacked the strangers instantaneously, even if all our warriors were there. We didn't have the Obi's mandate. We need your mandate, Your Majesty. If we see a war— any time, any day, anywhere – if we see a war, should we fight?

IGBOBA: Fight, loyal one, fight! Our gods and ancestors will protect you and all the warriors of Owa.

(EKOME *looks at* IGBOBA *in amazement while others chorus "Iseh!"* ONYELA *and* UZUN *kneel before* IGBOBA, *who touches them with his horse-tail whisk before they depart.*)

EKOME: Hmm! Obi Agun! You're mandating them to fight the white man? Hmmm! I think we should make peace with him-o.

IWEKUBA: Then go present yourself to the white man to be burnt as Owa's peace offering. One who burnt your gods and ancestors without qualms will gladly burn a cowardly young chief ... Wait. I'm hearing something ...

(*Everyone freezes as Town Crier's gong rises afar off, followed by the* TOWN CRIER'S VOICE:

Owa o Owa!
Open your ears and hear!
A rude foot has crushed the adder's tail
Open your ears and hear!
The leper you offered a handshake
Has invited you to bed – arms and legs open.

Owa o Owa!
Open your ears and hear!
Obi Igboba is singing
Open your ears and hear!

Nwa nw'ogbenyen Samara	[Orphan boy Samaran
Nwa nw'ogbenyen Samara	Orphan boy Samaran
Nni Oba sito Samaran	Food Oba cooked Samaran

E rikwe, e rikwe Samaran	Don't eat, don't eat Samaran
Oba tinye nsi o Samaran	Oba poisoned it Samaran
Oba tinye ejan o Samaran	Oba charmed it Samaran
K'ogbue y o Samaran	To kill you o Samaran
K'okwari uku y o Samaran	And take your inheritance Samaran]

Owa o Owa!
Open your ears and hear!

(Fade out lights and voice. A few moments later, lights on the townsquare. Enter CREWE-READ on a bicycle, with other members of his entourage running after him, including SGT. LAWANI, GILPIN, six CONSTABLES, OMOZEFI, JAMBA, AFOPELE, and some other RUNNERS/CARRIERS, carrying loads. CREWE-READ stops at the centre and alights from the bicycle. A carrier takes the bicycle from him and stands it at a corner.)

CREWE-READ: *(Astonished at the empty space.)* Good gracious! Sergeant!

LAWANI: *(At attention.)* Sir!

CREWE-READ: It's 5pm, isn't it?

LAWANI: *(Without checking.)* Yes, Sir!

CREWE-READ: Where is Owa?

LAWANI: Is a puzzle, Sir.

CREWE-READ: Unravel it.

LAWANI: Yes, Sir! *(Pointing at four RUNNERS.)* You, you, you and you, run to different quarters and drive the bloody baggers here. They cannot keep the white man waiting.

RUNNERS: Yes, Sir! *(They run off.)*

CREWE-READ: Sergeant!

LAWANI: Sir!

CREWE-READ: Where is Igboba?

31

LAWANI: Is a puzzle, Sir.

CREWE-READ: Now, this is really a puzzle. Igboba has been very time-conscious, just like us. It beats my imagination that he isn't here. What do you think, Mr Gilpin?

GILPIN: I smell a rat, Sir. Maybe insubordination, insurrection, insurgency, intrigue, indecorous incitement. Many words in the law books to describe his action, Sir, but the summary is, a rat. I smell a rat.

LAWANI: I quite agree with him in toto, Sir.

CREWE-READ: What could be the cause of that, Sergeant?

LAWANI: Is a puzzle, Sir.

CREWE-READ: Mr Gilpin?

GILPIN: I would say revenge, retaliation, reprobation, rebellion, revolution, reprisal for the attack on their jujus.

LAWANI: I quite agree with him in toto, Sir.

CREWE-READ: If that's what it is, then it is treason, a slap in the face of King Edward VII.

GILPIN: Otherwise called, treasonable felony.

CREWE-READ: Sergeant!

LAWANI: Sir!

CREWE-READ: Go and arrest Chief Igboba and drag him to my feet here.

LAWANI: Yes, Sir! (*Points at three constables.*) You, you and you, follow me! And bring handcuff.

CONSTABLES: Yes, Sir!

(*Exeunt LAWANI and the three CONSTABLES, after one of them had collected a pair of handcuffs from a carrier.*)

GILPIN: (*Chuckles.*) Arrest! And drag! (*Chuckles again.*)

CREWE-READ: What's that? (*No response.*) Mr Gilpin?

GILPIN: It's not important, Sir.

CREWE-READ: I still want to hear it.

GILPIN: Well, the DC can't be wrong, but I was just pondering over the protocol of indirect rule, Sir, vis-a-vis your order.

CREWE-READ: To hell with the protocol of indirect rule! Hasn't Igboba breached protocol by his action? By so doing, hasn't he voided his immunity? As a Court Clerk, you ought to know better, Mr Gilpin. The law is no respecter of persons.

GILPIN: If you say so, Sir.

CREWE-READ: What do you mean, if I say so?

GILPIN: Well, Sir, it's really not important, but I was just ruminating on whether rebellious Igboba would regard the law from your perspective, that is, with your own eyes.

CREWE-READ: I just can't see— (*Two* RUNNERS *run in, panting.* CREWE-READ *turns to* RUNNER I.) Yes?

RUNNER I: No people, Sir. Empty houses.

CREWE-READ: (*To* RUNNER II.) Yes?

RUNNER II: No peoples. Only lizards going to bed.

(CREWE-READ *paces the floor in puzzlement.* RUNNER III *runs in.*)

CREWE-READ: (*Charging at* RUNNER III.) Where are the people?

RUNNER III: Nobody, Sir. Only goats and sheep bleating *gbe-e, gbe-e* everywhere. (*Enter* RUNNER IV.)

CREWE-READ: Yes? Where's everybody?

RUNNER IV: Nobody to ask, Sir. The whole place is *weeeh*

like an abandoned farm road.

(*As* CREWE-READ *turns to* GILPIN *for an explanation, dissolve to Igboba's court.* IGBOBA *is standing before his throne, discussing in low tones with* ACHOLEM, IWEKUBA, NWOBI *and* EKOME, *who are standing before him. They are jolted by* LAWANI *and* CONSTABLES *making their entrance.* IGBOBA *hurries to sit on the throne as his chiefs and brother also take their seats one by one.*)

IGBOBA: (*After waiting in vain for royal greetings from* LAWANI *and his team.*) Yes, Sergeant?

IWEKUBA: (*Disdainfully.*) What's he sergeanting? Doesn't he know how to greet the king?

ACHOLEM: I wonder.

NWOBI: Why should he greet your king? The little bird dancing by the roadside has drummers underground.

EKOME: (*To* LAWANI, *conciliatorily.*) You are our own brother. Greet him "*Obi Agun!*" or "The King shall live forever!"

LAWANI: (*Expansively.*) There is only one king in United Kingdoms and British Dominions, including Owa. His name is His Majesty, King Edward VII—

NWOBI: (*To* ACHOLEM, *as* EKOME *returns to his seat.*) Didn't I tell you?

IGBOBA: I warn you, Sergeant: Don't ever say that again.

LAWANI: You can't warn me. By the authority of that one and only king of United Kingdoms and British Dominions, I have come to arrest you, Chief Igboba. So therefore, you are under arrest.

(IGBOBA *laughs for a while, then shakes his head in dismay.*)

NWOBI: My brother, the little dancing bird has drummers underground.

IGBOBA: What did you say, Sergeant?

LAWANI: You heard me well. You are under arrest.

IGBOBA: For what?

LAWANI: For insubordination, insurgency, insurrection, a rat, in short, for everything! (*Approaching the throne.*) You have right to remain silent—

IWEKUBA: (*Advancing menacingly towards LAWANI.*) It's your father that's under arrest, young man. Your father, your father's father, do you hear? It's your father's father's father that's under arrest.

LAWANI: Retreat or I shoot! (*Aims at IWEKUBA.*)

EKOME: (*Dashes to LAWANI.*) Don't shoot, I beg you—

IWEKUBA: Shoot!

(EKOME *dashes back, attempts to restrain* IWEKUBA, *who flings him aside and advances until the nuzzle of Lawani's gun is almost on his chest.*)

Shoot! I said, shoot! You bastard!

(*As* IWEKUBA *attempts to snatch his gun,* LAWANI *pulls back a bit and pulls his trigger. His gun doesn't explode.* IGBOBA *and* ACHOLEM *burst into laughter, but* EKOME *is still visibly scared.* NWOBI *rushes within.*)

Shoot again, fool! Aren't you a Bini man? Where is Ovonramwen, your Oba? If you knew how to shoot, why didn't you defend your Oba against the white man? Or do you only know how to team up with the stranger against your own people? (*Returning to his seat.*) Small-boy DC sent him, and he must come to arrest the Obi of Owa. Slave! He is pointing his gun at *me*, Iwekuba! Does he know Ekumeku? Does he think every stick is a gun?

LAWANI: (*Hurtles towards* IWEKUBA, *checks himself, then points his finger at him.*) You'll see. When the time comes, you'll see.

IWEKUBA: Go and eat shit!

LAWANI: Me?

ACHOLEM: Yes, go and eat shit, my boy. May I remind you that he just asked if you knew Ekumeku. Don't threaten those who are greater than you simply because you're carrying a stick.

IGBOBA: It's like the frog distending her belly in order to measure size with the cow. She'll end up bursting herself to shreds.

LAWANI: I agree with you in toto. But time will tell who is the cow and who is the frog in this matter.

(NWOBI *re-emerges. Almost immediately, youths of Owa, led by* ONYELA *and* UZUN, *invade the palace, some armed with cutlasses.* ONYELA *quickly deploys them strategically at the entrance of the court while he moves in with only* UZUN.)

You're wasting Government's time, Chief Igboba. Come down and follow me or I will move you by force.

IGBOBA: That's what I've been waiting for, my son. Come move your father by force.

LAWANI: (*Hands the gun over to* CONSTABLE I.) Give me the handcuffs.

CONSTABLE I: Yes, Sir! (*Produces a pair of handcuffs from his pocket.* LAWANI *and* CONSTABLE I *both move towards* IGBOBA.)

ONYELA: (*Orders* LAWANI *from behind.*) Don't you dare! (*Quickly gets to stand between* LAWANI *and the throne.*)

IWEKUBA: That's my boy!

LAWANI: (*To* ONYELA.) Vamoose or I arrest you.

ONYELA: Better to arrest me than my king.

IWEKUBA: He's just clattering his teeth. He can't arrest

anyone here.

LAWANI: At count of three: One ... two ... three! Now you are under arrest. Your hands.

(ONYELA *feigns to present his hands, but just before* LAWANI *handcuffs him, he snatches the pair of handcuffs from him, raises it as if to smash his head with it.* LAWANI *immediately snatches his gun from* CONSTABLE I, *repositions himself, and aims at* ONYELA, *but just before he pulls the trigger,* UZUN *cuts his arm with his cutlass and the gun falls.* LAWANI *clutches his bleeding arm.* UZUN *and* CONSTABLE I *scramble for Lawani's gun;* CONSTABLE I *gets it, and* UZUN *immediately takes to his heels.*)

Shoot the bagger!

(CONSTABLE I *shoots* UZUN *at the entrance of the court. He falls, writhes and dies. The other young men of Owa run off.* IGBOBA *blocks his own view with his hand, climbs down the throne and moves inwards, aided by* NWOBI *just as* EKOME *inches his way to the entrance and runs off.* IWEKUBA *shakes his head in utter dismay. The* CONSTABLES *overpower* ONYELA, *handcuff and drag him off. Dissolve to the narrators at the townsquare.*)

NARRATOR I: (*To* AUDIENCE.) Now you be the judge. Chichester, the District Commissioner on leave, for whom Crewe-Read was acting, could not have behaved like this. He worked as Assistant District Commissioner with Governor Ralph Moor during the Benin Massacre. Now as District Commissioner, he visited Igboba, and carefully explained to him how indirect rule worked. He respected the traditional institution, at least, in public. From what you've seen, ladies and gentlemen, what would you say was the matter with Crewe-Read?

(*Hands are raised in the audience, and the narrators recognize some people to speak, one after the other. NOTE: Narrators should give the first opportunities to members of the public audience and, like their traditional folktale performers, skilfully weave whatever they say into the process of the play. It is in the event that they do not speak that rehearsed MOA's are recognized.*)

MOA I: I think Crewe-Read was power-hungry and power-drunk.

NARRATOR II: Just like Vice-Consul Phillips, who, also in acting capacity, caused the Benin Massacre in 1897, and was beheaded by Bini warriors, along with six other white men in his company. (*Recognizes another* MOA.) Yes?

MOA II: Crewe-Read was pompous. He had a very low opinion of Blacks. He seized every opportunity to tell them how inferior they were to the white man.

MOA III: He was a racist.

MOA IV: He was young and inexperienced.

NARRATOR I: Though he sometimes claimed he was a Captain, British Army records show that he was only a yeoman in the Wiltshire Imperial Yeomanry during the 1900-1901 war in South Africa.

MOA II: What is yeoman?

NARRATOR I: A farmer who was used as a foot soldier when necessary.

NARRATOR II: (*To* AUDIENCE.) My people, whether he was a Captain or a yeoman, Crewe-Read was White. Every white man was wise enough to rule Blacks, *abi*?

NARRATOR I: So sad! ... Well, back to our story. Onyela was dragged to Crewe-Read's feet and Crewe-Read promptly dispatched him to Agbor prison.

The Middle

(*Dissolve to Crewe-Read's camp in the forest. About 9pm. Lanterns are hanging down the roof of the tent.* CREWE-READ *is sitting on a low stool, scribbling in a diary on his thigh. To his right,* GILPIN, *sitting on the floor, also scribbling on a paper in his file. To Crewe-Read's left,* LAWANI *is seated on the floor. A* CARRIER/RUNNER *is dressing his wound. Other* CARRIERS/RUNNERS *are seated all around while armed* POLICEMEN *are on guard.*)

GILPIN: (*Raising his head.*) Done, Sir.

CREWE-READ: Read.

GILPIN: (*Reads.*) From Ag DC, Agbor Sub-District to Provincial Commissioner, Central Province, Asaba. Insurgency Owa Agbor Sub-District Sgt Lawani wounded War imminent Reinforcements arms ammunition provisions needed urgently ADC and men camp Owa outskirts.

CREWE-READ: Good! Send the same to Officer Commanding, Central Army Command, Asaba.

GILPIN: Yes, Sir. (*Returns to scribbling.*)

CREWE-READ: Omozefi!

OMOZEFI: Sir!

CREWE-READ: Collect a powerful torch and get ready to run to Agbor with the telegrams. Instruct that they be dispatched tonight, for I'll issue order to march on Owa at 3 am.

OMOZEFI: Yes, Sir!

GILPIN: 3am, Sir? That's less than six hours from now. Would that be enough time for—

CREWE-READ: Mr Gilpin!

39

GILPIN: Sir!

CREWE-READ: The telegrams.

GILPIN: (*Shrugs.*) Here they are. (*Hands them over.*)

CREWE-READ: Omozefi!

OMOZEFI: Sir! (*Hurries to stand before* CREWE-READ.)

CREWE-READ: (*Hands over telegrams to him.*) Here. Run like a mad dog.

OMOZEFI: Yes, Sir! (*Puts the telegrams in his pocket, switches on his torch and runs off.*)

(*Blackout. Sound of "Iredi do"- pronounced "doh" - from afar:*

Iredi do, do, do	Iredi greetings
Iredi-o	Iredi
Onye gbu nw'eworo	Killer of lion's cub
Cheri nne-o	Wait for the mum
Ebelebe	Ebelebe

The song is repeated a number of times. Fade in frontage of Igboba's court. YOUTHS/WARRIORS *of Owa, in war attires, armed with guns, spears, bows and arrows, and sheathed swords strapped to the waist, are singing and dancing round the corpse of* UZUN. *At a signal from* EBIE, *singing stops and* WARRIORS *form a semi-circle with the corpse in front.*)

EBIE: (*Stepping forward, hails.*) Sons of the Lion!

WARRIORS: Yaa!

EBIE: Are you afraid?

WARRIORS: No!

EBIE: (*Louder.*) Sons of the Lion!!

WARRIORS: (*Thunderously.*) Yaa!!

EBIE: Yes. The lion cannot give birth to a lamb or a squirrel ...
    I thank you for having chosen me as your new leader

and chief warrior. I'm told the oracle has confirmed your choice and I want to assure you that I will perform.

WARRIORS: (*Hailing.*) *Mgborogwu!*

EBIE: That's me! The root that stabilizes the tree, the wrestler whose back never touches the ground! But, look ... (*Points to the corpse.*) ... Something has touched us, touched us like a needle in a sore. A son of the lion is down. His root has been cut. (*Declaims.*) Iredi! We are coming for you!

WARRIORS: Yes! (*They sing "Iredi do" again.*)

EBIE: We must take an oath now, not to let Owa down, not to let our king down, not to let our leaders down – arrested or slain. We must swear by the body and spirit of our slain leader. Are we ready?

WARRIORS: Yes!

EBIE: Now, everyone, kneel and place your weapon on him. (*They obey.*) Say after me: I swear by the body and spirit of Uzun—

WARRIORS: I swear by the body and spirit of Uzun—

(IWEKUBA *hurries in but stops on seeing the* WARRIORS.)

EBIE: That I will kill those who killed Uzun—

WARRIORS: That I will kill those who killed Uzun—

EBIE: And burn those who burnt our gods—

WARRIORS: And burn those who burnt our gods—

EBIE: And disgrace those who disgraced our king and chiefs—

WARRIORS: And disgrace those who disgraced our king and chiefs.

EBIE: Now, pick up your weapon and bite it. (*They obey.*) You may rise. (*As they rise,* IWEKUBA *comes closer.*) Father, why are you here? Must you follow me everywhere?

IWEKUBA: Why shouldn't I follow you? My mother followed

me everywhere, even to war. Sometimes, the enemy would fire at me and, *zaaam,* my mother would appear in front of me with her wrapper draping down her raised hands. The enemy's bullets would hit her wrapper and fall *katakata* to the ground. And my mother would disappear, *fiam!* (*Expressions of wonder.*)

EBIE: (*To* WARRIORS.) It's true. My grandmother told me before she died. But, Baba, no one has fired at me yet and you're not holding up any wrapper.

IWEKUBA: I've come to help. The Obi asked me to.

EBIE: Help with what, Baba?

IWEKUBA: To prepare the unprepared among you. They shot him (*Pointing to Uzun's body*) ... just once, with the same gun that went dumb when it was aimed at me! And here he lies lifeless. Some of you here came to that scene, and, when it was time to fight, you ran away! You can't go to war like that. And God forbid that you return like this ... (*Indicates the corpse.*) Owa is holding you like a priced bird and you cannot shed your feathers into her hands. So, those of you who know that, once they're shot, they'd fall like this, please, step out.

(*After a little hesitation, several people step out.* IWEKUBA *shakes his head in dismay.*)

You see what I mean? People don't win wars with songs and oaths only. I'll take these ones along to have them bathed and cooked while you bury the dead. Where will they meet you?

EBIE: The frontage of *ali,* the earth-god.

IWEKUBA: Very well. (*To those who stepped out.*) Follow me! (*As they move, a few more, who had not stepped out, run after them to the amusement of the others.*)

EBIE: (*After they had moved into the night.*) Thank you, Baba! What would I do without your support? (*Then to the remaining warriors.*) Take up the body and let's go.

(*As they bend to take up Uzun's body, dissolve to the frontage of Crewe-Read's camp. CREWE-READ and GILPIN are seated while LAWANI is drilling everyone else, all squatting on their toes, with the policemen in the front row.*)

LAWANI: Open hands behind your head; your fingers joined together. Like this ... (*He demonstrates.*) When I say "Up", you lift your body up a little, that is, lift your bottom away from your legs. When I says "Down", you lower your bottom. Like this ... (*He demonstrates.*) Up ... down ...; Up ... down ...; Up ... down ... You lift only your body, not your feet. Okay?

ALL: (*Except CREWE-READ and GILPIN.*) Yes, Sir!

LAWANI: Now, let's go. Up ... down; Up ... down; Up ... down; Up ... down; Up ... down; etc. (*They attempt to do as he commands, but not all get it right.*) All right! Shake it off, shake it off ... (*They rise and trot on the spot while at the same time stretching their legs, hands and necks at will.*) Atte-n-tion! (*They stand at attention.*) Now, you remember how to take cover when enemy fires at you?

ALL: Yes, Sir!

LAWANI: I'll test you now. At the count of three, I'll fire at you. You take cover or I blast your bloody head off. Okay?

ALL: Yes, Sir!

LAWANI: (*Points gun at chest level at the centre of their formation.*) One ... Two ... Three. (*Shoots. Some take cover; some squat; some fall awkwardly. Laughter. Then everyone is jolted as OMOZEFI runs in, panting. CREWE-READ and GILPIN spring to their feet.*)

CREWE-READ: What now?

OMOZEFI: (*Gesticulating wildly.*) They ... they ...

GILPIN: Who are "they ... they ..."?

OMOZEFI: I ... I ...

GILPIN: I thought you said "they ... they"?

OMOZEFI: I ... I reached Owa—

GILPIN: We are in Owa!

OMOZEFI: I mean Owa-Nta ...

CREWE-READ: And?

OMOZEFI: And ... and young men, dreadful like death ... they ... they came after my head—

GILPIN: And you ran back?

OMOZEFI: What ... what could *you* have done?

CREWE-READ: Disgusting!

GILPIN: Palpably preposterous!

CREWE-READ: Why did you run, Omozefi? They're your brothers!

OMOZEFI: But I'm ... I'm against them, Sir.

CREWE-READ: Nonsense! You weren't armed! And you are *not* a white man!

OMOZEFI: One of them identified me as Iredi's runner.

GILPIN: (*Murmurs aloud.*) This is why I advised against our camping here instead of returning straight to Agbor. Now we're marooned in this marquee.

CREWE-READ: Stop murmuring, Mr Gilpin!

GILPIN: I'm not murmuring, Mr ADC!

CREWE-READ: DC! (*Pause.*) I said, DC, Mr Gilpin!

GILPIN: Okay, DC. (*As if to himself.*) As if calling him DC would fight the war for us.

CREWE-READ: Pardon me.

GILPIN: I wasn't talking to you.

CREWE-READ: But I heard you ... Mr Gilpin, I said I heard you!

GILPIN: Okay, I'm sorry.

CREWE-READ: That's not enough!

GILPIN: Okay, I recant my words, Sir.

CREWE-READ: Better. Now get it straight into your skull that I won't hesitate to punish any insubordinate staff, be he Gilpin or Pingil. (*Louder.*) All of you, get that into your thick skulls, will you?

ALL: Yes, Sir!

CREWE-READ: Good. (*To* OMOZEFI.) Where are the telegrams?

OMOZEFI: (*Bringing them out of his pocket.*) Here, Sir. (*Hands them over.* CREWE-READ *is apparently not sure of the next step to take.*)

GILPIN: Sir, if it'd please you—

CREWE-READ: Nonsense, Mr Gilpin! What d'you mean, if it'd please *me*?

GILPIN: Sorry again, Sir. But, as you very well know, "if it'd please you" is an English manner of speaking ... If it'd please Mr DC, let's send Jamba. He's not known in this area.

CREWE-READ: Okay. But he'll go with Afopele, the son of Paramount Chief Imaran.

GILPIN: I don't mean to be obdurate or intransigent, Sir. But why must he go with Afopele?

CREWE-READ: He's committed.

GILPIN: And Jamba isn't, Sir?

CREWE-READ: Well, do you have anything against Afopele?

GILPIN: I'm just ruminating in my mind if you've studied him well enough, Sir.

CREWE-READ: Yes. I have. Very loyal. Haven't you noticed?

GILPIN: I have, Mr DC. He's so loyal that he almost licks your boots, Sir.

CREWE-READ: That's right. Besides, if the Owa-Nta rascals accost them and Afopele identifies himself, they'd certainly let them pass.

GILPIN: If you say so, Mr DC.

CREWE-READ: Jamba!

JAMBA: Sir! (*Runs from among the carriers/runners to* CREWE-READ. *She is actually* NARRATOR I *thinly disguised as a man.*)

CREWE-READ: Afopele!

AFOPELE: Yes, Sir! (*Also emerges from among the carriers/ runners. He is* NARRATOR II *also thinly disguised.*)

CREWE-READ: Get ready to run like a mad dog.

AFOPELE: (*Coming closer to* CREWE-READ.) Na true *Oga Oyinbo* talk! Gif me the telegrams, Sir. If I just stand like this *gidigba* (*Stands at attention, chest out.*) ... and say, Na mi bi Afopele, son of —

CREWE-READ: (*Makes to toss the telegrams into* AFOPELE's *hand, but changes his mind and tosses them into* JAMBA's *hand.*) Come on, run, you two!

JAMBA & AFOPELE: Yes, Sir!

CREWE-READ: (*As* JAMBA *and* AFOPELE *rush around to pick a few things.*) Hurry up! It's 12.30 am already and the telegrams must get to Asaba tonight.

AFOPELE: No bi Asaba? No worry, Sir. Me, I sabi run like

mad dog well well. (*He taps* JAMBA *and runs off.*)

JAMBA: (*As he follows* AFOPELE.) Please, pray for us.

GILPIN: We will. (*Turns to* CREWE-READ.) But, Sir, if I may ask again, is 3am still realistic for us to march?

CREWE-READ: I said 3am, and 3am it must be.

GILPIN: War isn't as simple as that, Sir.

CREWE-READ: I'm a Captain. What are you?

GILPIN: Court Clerk, Sir.

CREWE-READ: And what does Court Clerk know about war?

GILPIN: Absolutely nothing, Sir. But I'm just ruminating in my mind if the Captain has enough men and materials, enough arms and ammunition.

CREWE-READ: You know we've sent for reinforcements.

GILPIN: Would they come before 3am? Are we superlatively sure that the telegrams would have reached Agbor by 3am, let alone Asaba? ... Sergeant Lawani! Don't just keep mute. Please, advise him on—

LAWANI: I agree with Mr DC in toto. What do you know about war? What is your headache? Are you in command?

CREWE-READ: I think Mr Gilpin is beginning to show signs of disloyalty to His Majesty.

GILPIN: That's incredibly incorrect, Sir.

LAWANI: Then why are you arguing with the white man?

GILPIN: I'm not arguing with him. I'm advising him—

LAWANI: As what? Are you a white man? Who are you, common black monkey, to be advising a white man?

GILPIN: (*To* CREWE-READ.) I take exception to—

LAWANI: You can take exception to anywhere, I don't —

GILPIN: (*To* CREWE-READ.) Sir, can't you see that ... (*Points at* LAWANI.) he's the one being desperately disloyal to His Majesty and you? He ought to be advising you the way I'm doing. And to imagine that he's the one who'd face the enemy fire, since we don't have soldiers yet! To imagine too that it's *he* whose arm was cut some hours ago! Sergeant Lawani, you don't even love yourself.

LAWANI: How does that concern you, busybody?

GILPIN: It does concern me. I like to be my brother's keeper. In any case, just be sincere and advise Mr—

LAWANI: I'm not an adviser. I'm a policeman, a force man. I'm trained to take orders, not to advise.

GILPIN: (*To* DC *with a shrug.*) Maybe I should kowtow too— just take orders to prove my loyalty.

(CREWE-READ *does not respond. Dissolve to Igboba's court.* IGBOBA *has just picked up a spear from the shrine and is exercising his arm, making motions of throwing the spear. Enter* NNEKA, *about 90, tall, slim and still beautiful. She watches* IGBOBA *with admiration for some moments.*)

NNEKA: (*Hailing.*) Eworo! (*Pronounced "er-wor-ror" meaning "Lion"*)

IGBOBA: Hnmm!

NNEKA: Please, go to bed. The antelope shouldn't dance— break his legs before the public presentation of the dance. You need some sleep.

IGBOBA: Sleep! On a night like this?

NNEKA: All nights were created for sleep, My Lord.

IGBOBA: (*From now on, he punctuates his lines with his exercise with the spear.*) They were also created to harbour danger. That's why witches and wizards fly at night.

NNEKA: Do they?

IGBOBA: (*Casts a questioning glance at her.*) Are you asking me? Aren't you in a better position to tell me when and how they fly? Isn't your village the headquarters of witches and wizards in Owa kingdom?

NNEKA: Well, I asked you because we both know that, in your own village, they, I mean *all of you* – after all, you are one of them – you all fly in the afternoon as well.

IGBOBA: No time for your banters now, my queen. One whose house is on fire does not run after an escaping rat ... Tonight is particularly evil. Tell me why I should go to sleep. My sons are in the bush. Are they sleeping there?

NNEKA: It's past midnight, My Lord. You've kept sufficient vigil in sympathy with your sons in the bush. They'd sleep later this morning while you'd be holding court. This is a night of victory for us.

IGBOBA: You've come again, seer.

NNEKA: I can feel it.

IGBOBA: You always feel.

NNEKA: And I always feel right, don't I?

IGBOBA: You do, but go and feel in your room, you hear? I'll stay here till morning when, according to you, my sons can sleep.

NNEKA: I know what your problem is.

IGBOBA: Which is?

NNEKA: You wish you were the one leading our warriors in the battle.

IGBOBA: I really don't see why I shouldn't be—

NNEKA: Especially, since you're still full of energy, ehn?

IGBOBA: Am I not? (*Aiming the spear at her.*)

NNEKA: Of course, you are, my great lion! ... But lower

your spear or I'll go pick mine. You think I don't feel full of energy myself?

(IGBOBA *bursts into laughter as he lowers his spear.*)

Laugh, if you like … But, My Lord, what we feel now is a different kind of energy. It's energy to exist, energy to draw in air and hold on to life like a brittle string, energy to walk in the morning dew and yet convince yourself that you feel the heaviness of rain. It's the energy of a toddler's feet gripping the earth for fear of a fall. My Lord, it is not the same as the reckless energy that dares death. *That* is the energy needed to lead a battle. (IGBOBA *is suddenly depressed. Pause.*) Eworo! … E-wo-ro!

IGBOBA: (*Jolted.*) That's me!

NNEKA: Igboba of the lineage of deadly warriors!

IGBOBA: (*Now lighting up and prancing again.*) Eh-henn!

NNEKA: The descendant of Odogwu, the great warrior of the Benin Empire! The Crown Prince of Ute, who fought and fought for Benin until his own people thought he was dead and crowned his younger brother king!

IGBOBA: And when he finally returned, he did not call his younger brother a usurper and fight him.

NNEKA: Rather, he went afield and founded himself an even larger kingdom, this great kingdom of Owa!

IGBOBA: Oh, his magnanimity flows in my veins! And so does his valour!

NNEKA: The cat that taught the lion to hunt!

IGBOBA: That's me! Let the white man come. My blood is boiling *kutunku* like the deadly soup of the dead. Let the white man come. He calls us barbarians. So I will kill and eat him up!

NNEKA: Yes, you will. (*Pause.*) Do you remember what I

looked like when I was queen of the dance?

IGBOBA: How can I ever forget the succulence of your body, the suppleness of your waist, which lured me to marry before my mates?

NNEKA: Go! It was your sweet-mouth and long-throat that killed you!

IGBOBA: No, it was your beauty. You were beautiful everywhere and in everything!

NNEKA: Are you saying I'm no longer beautiful every—

IGBOBA: No, not exactly, I meant to say you ... ehm ... ehm ...

NNEKA: No need to stammer, My Lord. We're saying the same thing. Just as you wish you could still lead warriors to war, and kill and eat the white man, that's how I wish I could still lead the maidens in dance. That's how I still long to be queen of the dance. But where is the succulence

(NWOMA, *about 21, beautiful and very shapely, emerges from a side door, takes a quick impression of the scene, then hides in the doorway, peeping occasionally.*)

of my body now? Where is the suppleness of my waist? All gone! As strong as I seem, as elegant as I look, I can no longer dance those fiery waist dances that made you love me more than everyone else.

IGBOBA: Oh, don't make my mouth water!

NNEKA: I'm not talking about that kind of dance, you spoilt child!

IGBOBA: As if she wasn't the one who spoilt the child!

NNEKA: Seriously speaking, didn't you wonder why Iwekuba, a younger old man, retired from Ekumeku and from being our Chief Warrior? Didn't you wonder why he restrained himself from recklessly attacking the strangers who burnt our shrines? When I watched your stiff bones prance about with your spear, I understood why Iwekuba had to retire.

IGBOBA: Your tongue will kill you soon. You're calling me stiff bones, ehn?

NNEKA: (*Sighs.*) We all wish we could do this or that as we used to, but, since we can't cause the sun to remain permanently overhead, our sun sets unstoppably. It gets to a point when you call your muscles to duty and they stay limp; you call your waist and it doesn't answer; you call your joints and they stay stiff ... Go to bed, my one-and-only. At least, you still have energy to sleep.

NWOMA: (*Re-emerging.*) I knew it! (*To* NNEKA.) Look, if he's going to any bed tonight, it should be mine. You are not the only one who was queen of the dance. I was too. And he also chose me because of my natural endowments and my captivating waist-dance. If he must go to bed, it should be my bed. It is my turn tonight.

IGBOBA: There she goes again! People are saying what they're saying and Lizard springs up to say her daughter has no buttocks!

NWOMA: Who else could have said it for Lizard? Don't people speak only about their own problems? Perhaps, you think all I'm in this palace to do is pick your grey hairs. You cannot neglect me forever and continue to pour your treasures in the lap of one whose waist is already stiff.

IGBOBA: Don't be obscene, my daughter—

NWOMA: I'm *not* your daughter!

NNEKA: Our young queen, please, don't talk as if I'm competing with you for his ... his warmth. I'm not. A long time ago, my passion died with the stiffness of my waist.

NWOMA: Story! Why then were you inviting him to your bed? You think I didn't hear you?

NNEKA: I said he should go to his own bed!

NWOMA: What attracts him to your room so often? Why does he prefer your room to mine?

IGBOBA: Because I find peace there.

NWOMA: And you find war in my room, right?

IGBOBA: Isn't it war you're making right now? How many wars would I fight at a time? ... Listen to me, my sweet, young queen. Nneka discusses with me: issues of life, the governance of Owa, issues of growing old and death drawing close—

NWOMA: What's my business with all those?

IGBOBA: Exactly! You don't discuss. All you want is action, action, action, all the time. And when I call my waist and it doesn't answer, you flare up.

NWOMA: Why did you marry me if you knew your waist no longer answers your call? You married me to become your co-discussant? For two whole years after my delivery, you never came near my bed. Now that I've weaned my child, you still wish that, when you come to my bed, which you seldom do, I'd spend the time discussing with you? When will I make my babies, My Lord? I've just had the first one.

IGBOBA: You don't stampede to make babies.

NWOMA: So I'm stampeding, right? Ehn, let me stampede. (*Mimics.*) *I call my waist and it doesn't answer* ... Only when you're with me. In the arms of this ... (*Gestures at* NNEKA.) stiff waist, it answers. Yes, your waist answers when it sees her! Yet all her children, including the heir to the throne, are grown and established, safe from the white man's gun. You both can't deceive me anymore.

(IGBOBA *sneers at her and moves towards the door behind the throne.* NWOMA *dashes after him but screams and*

53

stops when IGBOBA *aims his spear at her.* IGBOBA *goes in and shuts the door.*)

NNEKA: Oh, see how she shivers with the cold of fear! Come, my dear. (NWOMA *runs into her arms and she holds her close for moments.*)

NWOMA: (*Slowly looking up to Nneka's face.*) Did he really want to kill me?

NNEKA: No, my daughter. He loves you so much that he couldn't have contemplated that. But this is war time. Anything can happen in war time.

NWOMA: (*Pushes off* NNEKA.) You can't scare me! Even he can't scare me. Indeed, that's what I need - his spear. Let him spear me tonight.

(NWOMA *dashes back to Igboba's door. As she begins to bang on the door, dissolve to* JAMBA *and* AFOPELE *as they emerge from the left side of the townsquare, running towards the right side. Suddenly,* AFOPELE *stops at the centre and sits on the ground, panting.* JAMBA *runs a short distance more before he realizes that he is running alone.*)

JAMBA: What's that?

AFOPELE: What?

JAMBA: What are you doing?

AFOPELE: Resting.

JAMBA: Resting!

AFOPELE: Erh-o! Resting.

JAMBA: The DC said the telegrams must get to Asaba tonight-o.

AFOPELE: Let them get to Asaba now. Am I stopping them? I must rest-o. Or did the Almighty DC say that Afopele, the son of Imaran, must die for the telegrams to get to Asaba? (*Pause.*) Come sidon, jor! Because DC don talk, we dey rush like dog wey death dey call. You no hear Omozefi? Owa-Nta dey wait to kill anyone from Iredi and we dey rush to go gif dem our neck! ... Make only you dey go sef. After all, na you be the Senior Courtma. 'E don tey wey you dey chop gofment money. So, na you 'e reach to die.

JAMBA: God forbid!

AFOPELE: Den sidon.

JAMBA: (*Sitting.*) But this is *insubordination*, erm ... *insurrection*, erm ... *insur* ... *insur-*

AFOPELE: If you like make you dey speak Gilpin grammar for der, make you de insur-anything wey you like. Me, I dey rest. Simple.

JAMBA: That's disloyalty to His Majesty's Service.

AFOPELE: Dat one na Iredi grammar. And 'e dey vex me well well: disloyalty to *Oyinbo* king wey I neva see for eye one day! And my own papa wey be king; dem com sey 'e no bi king again, 'e bi paramount chief, na'im be boi-boi to *Oyinbo* DC!

JAMBA: That's not the meaning of "paramount chief"!

AFOPELE: Make you dey deceive yourself for der. (*Stands, his mood changed.*) Just take a good look at me, Jamba, a prince that has become the white man's mad dog! I'll get to Owa-Nta and tell those warriors there with blood in their eyes ... (*Expansively*) "I am Afopele, son of Imaran, the paramount chief!" and they'd ... (*Demonstrates*) stand at attention, salute me and tell me to pass, hunn? Jamba, reason it now? If my father wasn't a traitor, would the white man have appointed him paramount chief? Did he appoint Ovonramwen or Nana a paramount chief? The warriors of Owa-Nta would see the son of a traitor running a traitor's errand for a white man and they'd tell me, well done? Mr Jamba, I'd be to them nothing more than a whiteman's dog with a telegram tied to its neck! And, if I were in their shoes, I'd cut off the mad dog's neck complete with the telegram on it! ... I'm angry now, Jamba. Very angry!

JAMBA: I can see that. Your mode of speech suddenly changed, your eyes are red, and you're trembling.

AFOPELE: Trembling with righteous anger. I am a prince and I went to school, Jamba, even though I've been doing *mumu* all this while ... I'm so angry I could kill you now!

JAMBA: (*Rising.*) Me? What have I done?

AFOPELE: Give me those telegrams at once!

JAMBA: It was *me* DC gave them to.

AFOPELE: I said, give me the telegrams!

JAMBA: No!

(AFOPELE *pulls out a jackknife from his pocket. JAMBA is shocked.*)

Ah-ah!

AFOPELE: Give them to me before— (*Raises the knife.*)

JAMBA: (*Hands the telegrams over.*) Here! (AFOPELE *tears them up, squeezes the pieces and throws them away, to the utter amazement of JAMBA .*)

AFOPELE: If you like, go back and report me to your small-boy *oyinbo* master. This is my opportunity to snatch my freedom from those who deposed my father and ruined my city. Right in front of us is Owa-Nta; behind us is Owa; to our left is the forest that leads to freedom. I'm going left, Jamba. You choose for yourself which way to go. (*Dashes into the centre aisle of the audience space.*)

JAMBA: (*After looking this way and that.*) Afopele! Please, wait for me! I'm coming with you!

(JAMBA *dashes into the centre aisle. Blackout. Gunshots*

56

from the direction of Owa. Moments after, lights on CREWE-READ's *camp. More gunshots. Panic in the camp.*)

CREWE-READ: (*Jumping to his feet.*) A bullet just swished past my ear!

GILPIN: They are dangerously close.

CREWE-READ: What do we do? Lawani!

LAWANI: Is a puzzle, Sir.

CREWE-READ: This is no time for puzzle.

GILPIN: He's not an adviser, remember?

CREWE-READ: (*Screaming.*) What do we do, Sergeant?

LAWANI: You give orders, Sir!

CREWE-READ: Damn you! Defend us! That's my order!

LAWANI: Order taken, Sir! Now, take cover, Sir! You and Mr Gilpin, while we return fire. Up, men! Get alert!

(*As the armed men jump to their feet, bullets hit two of them on the shoulder. They groan, clutch their shoulders and stoop.* CREWE-READ *crouches. In a jiffy,* GILPIN *fetches the bicycle and tosses it to* CREWE-READ.)

GILPIN: Get up and mount, Sir! (CREWE-READ *hesitates.*) Mount!

CREWE-READ: (*Obeys.*) To where?

GILPIN: (*Pointing towards Owa-Nta.*) This way! Pedal! Fast! (*Jolted by Gilpin's order,* CREWE-READ *fretfully pedals.*) Don't stay straight like a majestic tree! Take cover!

(CREWE-READ *bends low on his bicycle, pedalling as fast as he can.* GILPIN *runs after him.* CARRIERS/ RUNNERS *abandon their loads, except their torches, and run after* GILPIN, *everyone bent low.* LAWANI *and his men keep the rear. Though they occasionally fire back at the unseen enemy, they are virtually running with their backs. Spotlight on*

NARRATOR I *on the right side of the townsquare.*)

MOA I: (*Spotlighted in the* audience.) Will they escape?

NARRATOR I: You'll soon find out, my brother.

NARRATOR II: (*Spotlighted on the left side of the townsquare.*) Owa warriors pursued relentlessly. They bore no torches, but the moon showed them the way and the flickering torchlights of foolish, fleeing carriers showed them the enemy's location.

NARRATOR I: Crewe-Read rode his bicycle with all his might and those who ran after him ran, first like the hare, but then like the elephant! Occasionally, he looked back and waited for the elephants to catch up. He needed all the company he could get.

NARRATOR II: They ran, they ran. They ran for six miles and got to Owa-Nta. Two of Lawani's men had been killed and several others wounded. Their ammunition was almost exhausted and they could no longer return every fire. Their ankles squeaked and their hearts sank.

NARRATOR I: At last, it was dawn, a dewy dawn. Owa-Nta seemed deserted. That revived sinking spirits. Crewe-Read now pedalled like a majestic tree. In his mind, he and his men were making a triumphant entry into a conquered territory!

(*Lights on the left side of the townsquare as* CREWE-READ *and his party move in. Then spotlights on some* WARRIORS *in ambush in the forest, symbolized by a few front rows of chairs in the audience space. As soon as* CREWE-READ *rides to the centre, a* WARRIOR *fires a shot through his heart. He slumps to the ground and dies.* GILPIN, LAWANI, *the remaining* POLICEMEN, CARRIERS/RUNNERS, *stampede into the forest represented by the centre aisle.* WARRIORS *of Owa and Owa-Nta emerge from different directions and chase the escapees. As many of them are killed or wounded, moans and groans fill the air. Blackout. An instrumental rendition of "Fading away like the stars of the morning" rends the air. The volume is high for a while, then it softens but remains in the background. Fade on the Army Central Command Office, Asaba. CAPT. RUDKIN is studying a map on the wall. Among other things on his table is the British flag. Also on the wall is the framed photograph of King Edward VII. Two soldiers are on guard at the outside door. Enter CHICHESTER from a side door. The GUARDS turn immediately to salute him, then RUDKIN does the same.)*

CHICHESTER: It's a shame!

RUDKIN: (*Walking away from the map.*) Yes, it is. Just located Owa on that map. Care to sit, Sir? (CHICHESTER *virtually slumps into the seat. RUDKIN sits also.*)

CHICHESTER: It's awful too.

RUDKIN: Yes, it is. Tea or coffee?

CHICHESTER: None for me, thanks ... Who could have thought that, in a few days of my leaving Agbor Sub-District, everyone in Owa would become a monster? Head Chief Ektui - he's also called Igboba - was very hospitable, amiable, respectful and co-operative.

RUDKIN: Indeed? (*Glances at the outside door.*)

CHICHESTER: Oh, yes ... It beats my imagination how he automatically transformed into a rebel and a murderer in a few days. (*Pause.*) Maybe Lord Lugard was right when he described the African as an "excitable person, lacking in self-control, discipline and foresight ... full of personal vanity, with little sense of veracity". Or how else could one explain Igboba's leap into a war with His Royal Majesty, King Edward VII, without foreseeing the disaster that would definitely befall him and his people? How else could one explain his quick and easy breakage of his promise to me to keep the peace in my absence?

RUDKIN: What about the man, Crewe-Read? What was he like?

CHICHESTER: Young, ebullient, zealous, self-motivated. (*Pause.*) But I must confess I didn't feel comfortable handing over to him.

RUDKIN: (*Checks his time, then rises to glance at the door.*) Why, Sir?

CHICHESTER: Well, I'm a medical doctor by training and not a psychologist, but I had some uncanny feeling – and he did show signs of that, sometimes – that he could become overzealous and self-centred. Even overambitious.

RUDKIN: (*Checks his time, then glances at the door.*) It's easy to convert *zealous* to *overzealous* and *self-motivated* to *self-centred*, isn't it? I wouldn't hand over to him, if I were you.

CHICHESTER: (*Rising, as if stung, faces* RUDKIN.) That's if you had a choice! The bane of His Majesty's Service – as of Her Majesty's Service a few years back – is shortage of staff. Acute and chronic shortage of mature, experienced, well-trained staff. Such people prefer to remain in posh offices in the United Kingdom. Only the very adventurous ... Do you get me?

RUDKIN: Yes, Sir.

CHICHESTER: Only the very adventurous, the young and inexperienced, seeking an inlet into any respectable employment, only they cast caution to the wind and choose to confront the deadly mosquitoes of the rainforest: the anopheles, the Ologboseres, the Ekumekus, the Igbobas, all mosquitoes with their proboscides famished for the whiteman's blood.

(*End of instrumental music.*)

Blacks! They are opaque and unreadable, with hearts as deep as their jungles and as dark as their skin ... Sorry,

I'm garrulous and distracting you, apparently.

RUDKIN: Not exactly, Sir. I've been meaning to ask, did your own telegram come before mine?

CHICHESTER: No, the same E.C. Crewe-Read, twin brother of the slain man, brought yours and mine less than an hour ago. Why do you ask?

RUDKIN: We're having difficulty recruiting carriers for the expedition. All the young men of Asaba have gone to hide in the bush. How did they know of the revolt in Owa? How did they know we'd need them?

CHICHESTER: That shouldn't surprise you, Captain Rudkin. You know, of course, that the Ekumeku War, the uprising of the Western Ibos, which began in 1883, is still on. The leaders of the Ekumeku Movement have transformed it into an oath-taking cult. Every recruit into its infantry first takes an oath of secrecy. This makes it impossible for us to ascertain the Movement's source of power or information.

RUDKIN: Again, Blacks, deep and dark!

CHICHESTER: Yes. While Ekumeku remains inscrutable to us, it seems to have eyes and ears everywhere, within our own camps, even within our bedrooms! That, apparently, makes nonsense of Lugard's assertion that the African "lacks the power of organisation, and is conspicuously deficient in the management and control of men". Ekumeku does not only organize and control its members effectively, it also organizes and controls the entire Western Ibo citizenry. It disseminates important information to them before our telegrams arrive. It organizes even drums and gongs to function as runners or telephones!

RUDKIN: No wonder.

CHICHESTER: So what are you going to do? We must march

today.

RUDKIN: I know. I'm to command one and half companies of our regiment and they're good to go. But how do we go without carriers? I had to dispatch some soldiers to the streets to arrest and bring *anyone* found *anywhere* – indigenes and strangers alike. Anyone brought here would be conscripted into the carrierhood of His Majesty's Service.

CHICHESTER: Again, the problem of shortage of suitable staff! Untrained, unwilling, yet we conscript them! (*Looks at his wristwatch.*) I must go get set. See you soon.

(RUDKIN *salutes him and moves towards the front door. Dissolve to Igboba's court.* IGBOBA, NNEKA, NWOMA, ACHOLEM, EKOME, NWOBI *and* TOWNSPEOPLE *are celebrating.* MUSICIANS *are playing and* MAIDENS *are dancing while* WARRIORS, *apparently the guests of honour, seated on one side, are savouring the occasion. Most people are happy and drinking, though* IGBOBA, *as usual, is not drinking. Suddenly,* NWOMA *rises to whisper to* IGBOBA. *Apparently,* IGBOBA *doesn't support her proposition, but, after a brief unheard argument between the two,* NWOMA *casts off her outer attire to reveal her maiden dancer's costume. She takes to the dance floor, dazzles everyone with her virtuosity and becomes the cynosure of all eyes. Suddenly, she dances towards* EBIE *as if to engage him in dance.* EBIE, *flattered, dances a bit towards her.* IGBOBA *rises instantly as if in apprehension, but* EBIE *apparently disappoints* NWOMA *by kneeling before her with his head deeply bowed. As* NWOMA *veers off his way,* IGBOBA *steps down in a loud ovation, dances to meet her, hugs her, but, almost immediately, virtually pulls her by the hand back to her stool beside the throne. Two maidens dance towards* EBIE *while some others dance towards the other warriors. After a few moments of dance with the maidens,* EBIE *dances towards the drummers and, with special dance steps, halts the music. Frenzied ovation as* MAIDENS *retire to a corner*

62

opposite the position of WARRIORS.)

EBIE: (*Hails.*) Obi Agun! Reign forever!

ALL: Iseh!

EBIE: My elders and chiefs! I greet each one with his or her title!

(*They respond.*)

We're back.

ALL: Welcome-o!

EBIE: Thank you. We're here to formally tell Your Majesty that we've gone to the land of the dead to fetch the head of the king of the dead. (*Ovation.*) We've brought home the body of the king of lepers. (*More ovation.*)

IGBOBA: Well done, my son! When the kite swoops on his prey in a burning bush, does he get burnt?

ALL: No!

IGBOBA: My son, where's the body of the leper?

EBIE: We took it to the evil forest, My Lord, where lepers and other abominable souls rot.

IGBOBA: You're not only valiant but wise also. You are, indeed, true sons of Owa.

ACHOLEM: Your Majesty, may I remind us that Iwekuba is not here still.

IGBOBA: Don't worry. His son here is as good as he.

EBIE: My Lord, you're making my head swell! (*General laughter.*)

IGBOBA: But that's the truth. You've proved that the tiger doesn't give birth to a toad. And before the next farming season, we shall reward you and all the other warriors here with farmlands of your own.

(*In jubilation,* WARRIORS *kneel before the Obi, pay homage "Obi Agun!" and rise again. They also pay homage to the chiefs.*)

EKOME: When you appreciate the great farmer, his cutlass gets sharper.

IGBOBA: Oh, yes. (*To* WARRIORS.) We need to equip you to raise your own families. We hear that the nights of our maidens are now full of sweet dreams of you.

(*General laughter, which gets more animated as each warrior signals to a maiden to choose him and* MAIDENS *jokingly point accusing fingers at each other.* IGBOBA *raises a hand and there is silence everywhere again.*)

Since the farmlands we just promised you will take a few months coming, we shall give each of you an immediate reward.

EBIE: A maiden each?

(*Laughter.*)

ACHOLEM: It had better not be or all of us would become warriors at once!

IGBOBA: (*To* ACHOLEM.) At your age, what would *you* do with a maiden?

ACHOLEM: Give me the maiden first, my lord. And may I remind us—

EKOME: Remind, Reminder!

ACHOLEM: Yes, I'm Reminder. You are escapee. Run! Lawani's coming!

(*Laughter.*)

May I remind us ... may I remind us that there's someone here who's much older than me, whose maiden wife just weaned a child.

(*Laughter.*)

IGBOBA: (*Enjoying the joke.*) Name the person, Iyase.

ACHOLEM: Me, name the person? This frail tongue of mine, can it lift such a great and mighty name? My Lord, we all know the person but it's not me that will name him in the open. All I'm saying is that the hen may have no teeth but it easily eats *akamkpo*, the tough, dry corn.

(*More laughter.*)

IGBOBA: Well, I don't know what Iyase is talking about. But, my warriors, here's your immediate reward. You go to our oil palm reserve on the next *Afor* day, which is the day after tomorrow, and harvest for yourselves as many ripe palm bunches as you can!

(*Wild jubilation. WARRIORS troop to kneel before the Obi. Five young men, STRANGERS, run in and also fall on their knees, then they rise with WARRIORS, who turn around and are amazed to see them.*)

WARRIORS: (*In unison, menacingly.*) Who are you?

IGBOBA: Easy with them, great warriors.

EBIE: They might be spies, My Lord.

IGBOBA: We'll know when they open their mouths.

NWOBI: (*To STRANGERS.*) Young men, let's hear you.

STRANGERS: (*Kneeling again.*) Obi Agun! May you live long for us to serve!

ALL: Iseh!

NWOBI: You're our people then?

STRANGER I: Yes, my Elder. From the palace of Agbor.

IGBOBA: Oh, from my brother king! How's he?

STRANGER I: He's fine, Your Majesty.

IGBOBA: And the people of his kingdom?

STRANGER I: We are all fine.

IGBOBA: How are my brother king and his people relating to the white man?

STRANGERS: Very well indeed.

NWOBI: He must be treating your kingdom very well then.

STRANGERS: Yes, my Prince. (IGBOBA *pouts*.)

STRANGER I: (*After a pause*.) Obi Agun! May you live long for us to serve!

ALL: Iseh!

STRANGER I: We are messengers, and the message does not kill the messenger.

EBIE: It depends on the message and the tact of the messenger.

IGBOBA: Go on, boy.

STRANGER I: The palace of Agbor requests that you release his body to us.

IGBOBA: Whose body? ... Ebie!

EBIE: Obi Agun!

IGBOBA: Did you kill an indigene of Agbor and carry away his body?

EBIE: No, My Lord.

IGBOBA: (*To* STRANGER I.) Whose body do you want, young man?

STRANGER I: It's not we, Your Majesty. It's the palace —

ACHOLEM: Whose body does your palace want?

STRANGER I: The body of Iredi, the white man.

IGBOBA: Iredi?

STRANGERS: Yes, My Lord.

IGBOBA: Which quarter in Agbor is his father from?

STRANGER I: His father?

IGBOBA: Yes, his father. People demand the bodies of their relatives to take them home for burial. In which quarter in Agbor did Iredi have relatives?

(*No response.*)

Young man! Be truthful! It's not the palace of Agbor that sent you. It's the white men acting through your palace. (*Pause.*) And our message to them is this: If they want Iredi's body, let them come for it. Have you heard?

STRANGER I: (*Defiantly.*) But we were instructed not to return without the body.

EBIE: (*To* STRANGER I.) True?

STRANGER I: Yes.

EBIE: (*Bowing deeply to* IGBOBA.) Obi Agun! Permit us to take them to Iredi's body.

ACHOLEM: What?

EBIE: Yes, my Iyase. Since Iredi went there, he hasn't returned and these ones have also been ordered not to return. Perhaps, Iredi needs carriers even in death. (*To* WARRIORS.) Sons of the Lion!

WARRIORS: Yaa!

EBIE: Sons of the Lion!

WARRIORS: Yaa!

EBIE: Take them to their master.

(WARRIORS *burst into the Iredi song, seize the strangers and begin to drag them off.*)

IGBOBA: (*Declaims.*) Sons of the Lion! (*To* TOWNSPEOPLE.) Stop them!

(*Some* TOWNSPEOPLE *stop them.*)

IGBOBA: Sons of the Lion!

WARRIORS: Obi Agun!

IGBOBA: Let them go.

EBIE: Obi Agun, you mean—

IGBOBA: Release them! Now!

(*As* WARRIORS *lose their hold on them,* STRANGERS *run off to the amusement of all. Dissolve to District Commissioner's office at Agbor. It has two tables, one executive and the other non-executive. A British flag on the executive table, a map on the wall and a steel filing cabinet in a corner.* GILPIN *is seated by the non-executive table, scribbling. Enter* CHICHESTER. GILPIN *stands.*)

CHICHESTER: How d'you do?

GILPIN: How d'you do too, Sir? Glad to see you again, Sir.

CHICHESTER: You should be. I escaped death by a whisker. Those Ekumeku warriors are horrible! Lt Walmsley-Dresser is out there on a hammock borne by some carriers. He's badly wounded on the chest and legs.

GILPIN: Oh, dear!

CHICHESTER: Take him to the sick bay. He should be treated at once.

GILPIN: In a jiffy, Sir. (*Makes to go.*)

CHICHESTER: Mr Gilpin!

GILPIN: Sir!

CHICHESTER: No Ekumeku must know where he is. Is that clear?

GLIPIN: Yes, Sir. (*Makes to go.*)

CHICHESTER: Well, that reminds me: I've never asked you

where you come from.

GILPIN: That's a long story, Sir. May I attend to the wounded first?

CHICHESTER: Mr Gilpin!

GILPIN: Sir!

CHICHESTER: Are you Ekumeku?

GILPIN: That's luxuriantly ludicrous, Sir. But, if I were, I won't say "yes". No serving Ekumeku owns up.

CHICHESTER: Be straight, Mr Gilpin! We don't have time. Are you Ekumeku?

GILPIN: No, Sir!

CHICHESTER: Gilpin ... Is that your true name?

GILPIN: Yes, Sir.

CHICHESTER: From where? One word!

GILPIN: Koko.

(CHICHESTER *rushes to the map on the wall to locate Koko.*)

CHICHESTER: Koko, the place of Nana of Itsekiri?

GILPIN: Yes, Sir! No Ekumeku there, Sir.

CHICHESTER: Go.

GILPIN: You can trust me, Sir. What's more, my grandfather was British like you, one of the early traders across—

CHICHESTER: I said, GO!

GILPIN: Yes, Sir! (*Exits.*)

(*Dissolve back to Igboba's court. Everyone else is gone except* IGBOBA, ACHOLEM, EKOME, NWOBI *and the* WARRIORS, *some of whom are still drinking.* IWEKUBA *rushes in.*)

IWEKUBA: Obi Agun! Have you been told?

IGBOBA: What?

IWEKUBA: Who were those men? The young strangers running off as I was on my way here.

IGBOBA: Young men from Agbor sent to retrieve Iredi's body.

IWEKUBA: They'd soon have more whitemen's bodies to retrieve. We've just fought the baby battle; the mother battle is approaching fast.

(*Sounds of amazement or horror.*)

MOA: From where?

IWEKUBA: They'd have crept on us last night; they'd have overwhelmed us like sinister ants on defenceless chicks!

MOA: Who?

IWEKUBA: White men! White Army Officers, leading Black soldiers, carriers, runners, very many people!

NWOBI: No wonder the endless shooting of last night.

IGBOBA: But it sounded very far off.

IWEKUBA: Umunede bush, Your Majesty! Next door! Ekumeku warriors intercepted them on their way to Owa. All through the night, they fought them.

IGBOBA: Good! My ancestors will always raise an army to ambush my enemies! They'll never get to Owa!

ALL: Iseh!

IWEKUBA: But, My Lord, they broke through Ekumeku just before dawn. They are marching furiously to Owa.

IGBOBA: Are you sure of—

IWEKUBA: Your Majesty, true that I retired from Ekumeku a few years ago, but my ears and eyes are still with them. The whiteman's army is marching furiously to Owa as we speak.

IGBOBA: Let them come!

IWEKUBA: But I must tell you some White army officers are already bleeding in their chests. Encountering Ekumeku in the bush is not like meeting a shy girl in a bush path.

IGBOBA: I said, let them come. Owa will finish what's left of them. Is the finger nail scared of scabies?

IWEKUBA: No!

IGBOBA: Sons of the Lion! Is the finger nail scared of scabies?

WARRIORS: No!

IWEKUBA: (*To* WARRIORS.) A scheduled fight, does it consume the cripple?

WARRIORS: No!

IWEKUBA: But the cripple must start off early, not so?

WARRIORS: It is so.

IWEKUBA: Drop your cups then, and follow me.

(*Exeunt* IWEKUBA *and* WARRIORS. *Fade in* NARRATORS.)

NARRATOR II: The Ekumeku encounter was on the night of June 13, 1906. For twelve hours, the battle raged.

NARRATOR I: After Lt Walmsley-Dresser was demobilized by Ekumeku, Captain Rudkin had only one professional combatant army officer left with him — Lt H.C. Fox. The other two army officers, A.A. Chichester and J.B. Bate were essentially medical personnel. So Captain Rudkin had to wait in Umunede bush for reinforcement before proceeding to Owa.

NARRATOR II: He left Asaba June 11, 1906, with 180 African rank and file and 54 unwilling carriers and 20 more from Iselle-Uku.

NARRATOR I: (*Hailing* NARRATOR II) Master of dates and figures!

NARRATOR II: Thank you, my sister. Rudkin lost nearly twenty per cent of those numbers to Ekumeku at Umunede.

NARRATOR I: Owa was waiting, spoiling for a fight!

NARRATOR II: On June 15, Capt. J. Wayling and Capt. L.O.W. Jones arrived Umunede with additional 150 troops. Lt Hopkinson also joined them with a small party of rank and file before dusk.

NARRATOR I: At nightfall, after they had rested, Rudkin announced the plan.

(*Dim spotlight on* RUDKIN *in front of a tent in his camp in Umunede bush, represented by Crewe-Read's camp. Martial music in the background.*)

RUDKIN: (*Addressing an imaginary parade of troops.*) Column 1, under the command of Capt. J. Wayling, shall march South to Agbor. There, you'll meet Acting Provincial Commissioner A.A. Chichester. He was in the Egyptian war of 1885 as navy on board Her Majesty's Hospital-ship. He had worked as Assistant District Commissioner with Governor Ralph Moor in Benin during the Benin Massacre. Now, he has the mandate of the Home Office to quell the revolt in Owa. So, he is our boss, technically. He will guide you from Agbor, across some villages, to Owa. Column 2, under my command, shall go North-East to Otolokpo, to Ute, to Owa. We shall attack Owa from two flanks at the same time. But we must first carefully locate the enemy position before we attack. With the field telephones which Capts. Wayling and Jones kindly brought, I'll co-ordinate our moves. Is that clear?

VOICES/MOA: Yes, Sir!

RUDKIN: We leave two detachments behind. The one

commanded by Capt. L.O.W. Jones shall remain here while the one commanded by Lt Hopkinson shall stay at the Agbor base. They shall provide reinforcements when needed. Understood?

VOICES/MOA: Yes, Sir!

RUDKIN: Good luck!

VOICES/MOA: Good luck, Sir!

(Blackout. Martial music rises, tarries for a few moments, then dissolves into an Owa war song, which also rises, tarries for moments, and fades. Lights on District Commissioner's Office. CHICHESTER, in army officer's uniform and holding a swagger stick, is sitting on his table.)

CHICHESTER: *(After looking at his wristwatch.)* All's set, Mr Gilpin. We'd depart any moment from now. What's your advice?

GILPIN: Crewe-Read taught me to take orders and not to advise, Sir.

CHICHESTER: Come off it! I'm not Crewe-Read.

GILPIN: But, yesterday, you sounded like him, Sir - brashly draconian, shouting at me, "Be straight!" "Answer, ONE WORD!" You even insinuated I was Ekumeku!

CHICHESTER: I'm sorry, Mr Gilpin, but I'm sure you'd have done the same, if you were in my shoes. Everything that I knew around here changed so fast. Imagine what Head Chief Ektui has become!

GILPIN: But that's the point, Sir. Insurrection is often induced by racism, arrogance, high-handedness and insensitivity. Crewe-Read was guilty of all—

CHICHESTER: Speak no ill of the dead.

GILPIN: Yes, I won't, Sir. That's why I described him exactly as he was. He knew *everything* and never considered anyone's advice.

CHICHESTER: Again, I'm not Crewe-Read. What's your advice to me?

GILPIN: Go to war.

CHICHESTER: Against my very hospitable, very respectful friend?

GILPIN: Sir, you began this conversation with "All's set, Mr Gilpin. We'd depart any moment from now". Sir, with all due respect, should Mr Gilpin's advice unset all that's set or stop you from departing any moment from now? A trite law is expressed thus: *Audi alteram partem,* which means, you must hear from both parties before making a judgment. Permit me to ask, with all due respect, have you heard from your "very hospitable, very respectful friend"?

CHICHESTER: What kind of question is that, Mr Gilpin? You yourself wrote the telegrams that we read. Through the telegrams, we knew what transpired.

GILPIN: I told you, Sir, that I obeyed orders. I wrote telegrams for those who signed them. I said what they ordered me to say. The telegrams expressed the mind of the white man. With all due respect, Sir, did you receive a telegram from Chief Igboba?

CHICHESTER: This is damnable! Earlier, I asked if you were Ekumeku; you said you weren't. Now you speak like their advocate. Exactly on whose side are you, Mr Gilpin?

GILPIN: On the side of justice, Sir. Working in the court of law these many years has taught me to be on the side of jus––

CHICHESTER: You're suspect, Mr Gilpin.

GILPIN: Suspect!

CHICHESTER: Yes.

GILPIN: Well, Crewe-Read called me worse names, Sir.

But such is life. If someone made up his mind prior to seeking your advice, whatever you say that contradicts his mind makes you his enemy. Hence I said, go to war, Sir. I'll be praying for your safety. No matter what, you are a good man, a much better man than Crewe-Read.

CHICHESTER: Thanks for your compliment. (*Glances at his watch again.*) I must go now.

(CHICHESTER *moves outwards. Then fade in* EBIE *in a hazy spotlight, addressing an imaginary formation of warriors.*)

EBIE: Sons of the Lion!

VOICES/MOA: Yaa!

EBIE: My father said they left Umunede and Agbor this morning, and should enter Owa by different routes by nightfall. We, in Owa, shall be like the sun; the warriors from surrounding villages shall be like the boarders of the halo of the sun. The enemy troops shall be allowed to come in through the boundaries, and when they are in-between the sun and the boundaries of its halo, rays from the sun shall hit their faces and rays from the halo shall hit their backs. Understand?

VOICES/MOA: Yaa!

EBIE: Remember we are on oath. Any lion that fights with the heart of a chicken or tries to run away like a baby goat or betrays Owa in any way shall eat sand. Understand?

VOICES/MOA: Yaa!

EBIE: Our gods and ancestors will go with us.

VOICES/MOA: Iseh!

EBIE: Obi Agun says "Iyare!" We shall go and return.

VOICES/MOA: Iseh!

(*Blackout. Lights on the palace.* IGBOBA *is seated on the throne, speaking onto a round object, the size of a kola nut.* DIBIE, *with a white-chalk ring round his left eye and wearing a red, flared skirt with white stripes, is standing close to* IGBOBA. ACHOLEM *is seated on a bench to Igboba's right;* NWOBI *is seated on a bench to his left; between them, on the floor, is Dibie's mat with his instruments of divination, consisting of what is locally called igbagba efa and its seeds. Igbagba efa is like a round, thick pad with a depressed middle upon which divination seeds are packed. It also has a round, padded cover with a handle.*)

IGBOBA: What to do that the visitor will not kill his host. What to do that he that I did good to will not pay me with evil. What to do that this war will be mere breeze to Owa, mere dew.

(IGBOBA *hands the object back to* DIBIE, *who goes to sit on his mat. Witchdoctor's drumbeats. With the round object,* DIBIE *touches the divination seeds, packs them from the mat unto the pad, raises the pad cover from the floor and slams it over the seeds.*)

DIBIE: Igbagba! Speak, for our ears itch!
What to do that the visitor kill not his host
That the dew drench not your people to death
That water, water that we drink stick not in our teeth

(*Raises the igbagba cover, studies the seeds briefly, and slams the cover on the pad. Lifts the cover and studies the seeds again.*)

Igbagba! It's you I call!
Do not learn dumbness at old age
The dumbness of the duck fills the hawk with fright

(*Enter* EKOME *in haste. He sits without saying anything to anyone.*)

Speak! Igbagba, Speak!

Speech that would soothe troubled hearts

(*Packs up the seeds, casts them again on the igbagba-efa, slams the cover on them, lifts the cover, studies the seeds intently, then raises his head, contemplating, his brows knitted.*)

IGBOBA: (*Somewhat relieved.*) They seem to have spoken at last! Voice of the gods, what did they say?

(*No response.*)

Whatever it is, let me hear it.

NWOBI: Dibie! The Obi is asking you!

ACHOLEM: May I remind you, Dibie, that you just asked the oracle not to learn dumbness at old age.

DIBIE: Cripple!

IGBOBA: Yes? Cripple.

NWOBI: What should we do with a cripple? Sacrifice him or what?

DIBIE: Cripple in a desolate place! Everywhere *weey* like the road to the evil forest!

IGBOBA: What do you mean?

DIBIE: It's not me, My Lord.

NWOBI: Then what do they mean?

DIBIE: What they told me is what I've spoken.

EKOME: Cripple! That's all they found to say? Then who cannot be a god, if all you need say when your worshippers present before you their life-threatening problems is "Cripple"?

IGBOGBA: Well, Dibie, we heard you. Your oracle said "Cripple in a desolate place". You'll leave us to ponder over that. Thank you so much.

(DIBIE *packs his things and leaves*. IGBOBA *turns to* EKOME.)

IGBOBA: Welcome, my chief. How was your journey?

EKOME: My Lord, was that a journey?

ACHOLEM: No wonder you stayed a whole day longer.

NWOBI: I was beginning to wonder if Igbogiri had moved to a farther place.

EKOME: Thorns in my way, everywhere I turned!

IGBOBA: The oracle of Igbogiri—

EKOME: Oracles, My Lord. I consulted three!

IGBOBA: Better! What did they say?

EKOME: Hmm, My Lord. I wonder—

IGBOBA: No time to wonder now. Just break the word *dai*. What did they say?

EKOME: The first one said nothing.

IGBOBA: What do you mean nothing?

EKOME: The diviner merely raised his head and said to me, "Greet your Obi".

ACHOLEM: Greet your Obi!

EKOME: Yes.

MOA: Did you tell him your Obi fell from a palm tree?

EKOME: Ask me, my brother.

IGBOBA: And the second one?

EKOME: The second and the third one did the same thing.

IGBOBA: Which was?

EKOME: They sang a song.

OTHERS/MOA: Song!

78

EKOME: Yes, song.

IGBOBA: What song?

EKOME: "Imina". That "Imina" song.

(Everyone is nonplussed and agape. The "Imina" song swells up and overwhelms the place as everyone freezes:

Mm mm mm mm Imina	Mm mm mm mm Imina
Oh oh oh oh Imina	Oh oh oh oh Imina
I buche eka im'ite	To dip hand in pot Imina
A fun'orun Imina	Is not hard Imina
Ite om'ahun	That beautiful pot
Wu kwo nke nmo-o	Is for the dead
Imina awa wa wa	Imina awa wa wa
Imina nwa m-o	Imina my child
Imina oko ko ko	Imina oko ko ko
Imina nwa m-o	Imina my child-o
Imina-o	Imina-o.

(Fade out lights with the song. A few moments after, spotlight on NARRATOR I. MOA I, also spotlighted, raises a hand.)

NARRATOR I: *(Seeing the raised hand.)* Yes, please.

MOA I: Who is the cripple, the cripple in a desolate place?

(Spotlight on MOA II, also raising a hand.)

NARRATOR I: *(Recognizing MOA II.)* Yes, please.

MOA II: Who has dipped his hand in the pot of the dead?

NARRATOR I: My people, all I can say is that darkness was approaching. For the answers to your specific questions, maybe I should go consult the oracles. Maybe they'd explain everything to me because I'm a beautiful lady!

(Blackout. Then lights on Iredi's tent. In front of it, corpses of three White soldiers and two sentries standing beside them. CHICHESTER is leaning against a tent pole with chest bandaged. BATES pulls a syringe out of his arm.)

79

BATES: Your pains would soon subside and you'd be able to sleep.

CHICHESTER: Thanks. But (*Pointing*) ... those gallant soldiers died in your hands?

BATES: Just one.

CHICHESTER: You mean one out of three is a good number to lose? I'm scared.

BATES: He was almost dead on arrival. You're a medical doctor like me, I was told. So, trust me, Sir.

CHICHESTER: Of course! But ... are we going to leave their corpses here for the Black vultures to feast on?

BATES: They were many more corpses actually—

CHICHESTER: Whites?

BATES: Both colours but many more of Blacks. About a ratio of one White to eight Blacks.

CHICHESTER: Yet there are three Whites down there and no Blacks?

BATES: You need to rest, Sir. Or should I administer another dose of—

CHICHESTER: I'm loquacious by nature. But just answer me that before I fall asleep. I'm almost there.

BATES: Well, carriers have been quite busy removing the many corpses, perhaps, indiscriminately. And, as you know, Sir, we lost many carriers and one or two out of our five hammocks.

CHICHESTER: Dr Bates, you brought just *five* hammocks?

BATES: There were tons of other more essential supplies to carry, Sir. And, well, who expected this number of casualties?

CHICHESTER: (*After a brief pause.*) Dr Bates.

BATES: Not sleeping yet, Sir?

CHICHESTER: Why do they always aim at our chests? They shot Crewe-Read in the chest, Walmsley-Dresser in the chest, two of those three in the chest, and now, me. Who told them the location of the heart?

BATES: Anatomy.

CHICHESTER: Natives! Anatomy?

BATES: (*Unfolds a light mattress and places it on the ground.*) You need rest, Mr Chichester. Here, please.

(CHICHESTER *hesitates, then, as he lies down,* CARRIERS *run in with a black wounded soldier in a hammock, groaning in pains. One of them fretfully whispers to* BATES *and* CHICHESTER. *They drop the hammock with the Black wounded soldier beside the dead White soldiers.* CHICHESTER *attempts to rise but can't. Quickly, they lay the Black soldier on the ground, lift* CHICHESTER *into the hammock and the hammock onto their shoulders, and vamoose into the dark with* BATES. *On their trail, gunshots, groans and moans for moments. Twilight on the road, represented as before by the townsquare. Some soldiers are escaping from Owa-Nta and running towards Owa, majority of them bleeding, a few without arms or clutching their wounds. Every gunshot jolts them visibly. Fade in* NARRATORS, *watching them escape.*)

NARRATOR II: That was June 17. The battle was fierce.

NARRATOR I: Very fierce.

NARRATOR II: Only the wounded were brought in with the hammock.

NARRATOR I: They also brought in the dead, if they were Whites.

MOA: And if they were Blacks?

NARRATOR I: They were left in the cold arms of the forest.

81

There weren't enough hammocks and carriers for Blacks. Which is why Chichester found only White corpses.

NARRATOR II: On that day, June 17, two rank and file were killed, six severely wounded, and 20 slightly wounded. Dr Bates was stretched to breaking point.

NARRATOR I: Yet, that was really the beginning. Major battles lay ahead.

NARRATOR II: By July 2nd, half of Rudkin's troops were casualties. Then the remaining half adopted new tactics: advance, strike ... (NARRATOR I *joins in*) ... and retreat. Advance, strike —

MOA, AUDIENCE: —and retreat!

NARRATOR II: The warriors of Owa didn't suspect that white men also play tricks like the tortoise. So, when they retreated, many warriors of Owa thought they had run away. They looked at the countless corpses of the White man's soldiers on the ground and said, "Who could blame them for running for their dear lives?" But the tortoises drifted back like a silent wave and attacked Owa warriors at rest. They killed some.

NARRATOR I: Advance, strike—

MOA/AUDIENCE: —and retreat!

NARRATOR II: Suddenly, it seemed as if the whiteman's army had retreated finally. Several days passed and no one advanced; no one struck; no one retreated. The silence was thick and pitch dark.

(*Blackout. Then twilight on* WARRIORS *of Owa at a rectangular yam clearing simulated by the townsquare.* EBIE *is addressing them.*)

EBIE: We've done well. We've almost finished them. They killed some of us – that's how life is; a war must take lives — but we can count the number that we lost with our fingers, and we didn't leave anyone to rot in the bush or be feasted on by vultures the way they left their dead, Black soldiers. Everyone we lost was taken home for a decent burial. Sons of the Lion!

WARRIORS: Yaa!

EBIE: Yes, we've done well. But I cannot deceive you: they dislodged us too soon, made us huddle together, made us stand like a wrestler with his two feet tied together. That's why I summoned you all here. Do not be deceived, my brothers: their disappearance is like the squat of the cat. The squatting cat pounces when you least expect. We must re-strategize now. We must mend the halo that they broke. That halo formation yielded our initial victory over them, and we must recover and sustain that victory. Sons of the Lion!

WARRIORS: Yaa!

(*A gun explodes from the South.* WARRIORS *instinctively drift northward, but a shot comes from there also.* WARRIORS *drift to the west. Another gunshot from there veers them eastward only for them to also encounter a gunshot from the east. They huddle together, then spread out to form a little square with their backs to the centre and their faces to the advancing troops, their guns and bows ready. Rudkin's troops advance, somewhat confidently, from the four corners, their guns also ready.*)

EBIE: (*Suddenly.*) Sons of the Lion!

WARRIORS: Yaa!

EBIE: What's your choice: to kill or be killed?

WARRIORS: Kiiiill!

EBIE: Then kill!

(*The rest of the encounter is in choreographed mime and slow motion to the accompaniment, in the background, of both Western martial music and African war drumbeats as well as intermittent sounds of gunshot.* WARRIORS *spread* out further in four directions to tackle the advancing enemy, firing and receiving fire in mime. Casualties drop on all sides. Some, seriously wounded, fall and groan. Soon, WARRIORS begin to lose steam as Rudkin's troops come in waves, increasing in number due to reinforcements, and exhibiting greater fire power. Suddenly, EBIE mimes a loud signal and heads in a direction. At once, WARRIORS follow him, charging desperately. They break through the particular flank they charged against, felling some whiteman's soldiers in their way. Some WARRIORS are killed in the process but many escape, unpenetrated by bullets, though still being chased by some of their enemies. End of African war drumbeats. A few wounded WARRIORS are held to the ground, handcuffed and brought before RUDKIN. As they are led away by RUDKIN and his men, "Imina" wells up to drown marshal music.)

The Ending

(*Lights on Igboba's court. IGBOBA and NWOMA are by the entrance to the court, looking out. Soon, EBIE and two other WARRIORS are seen running towards the court. Song fades to the background.*)

NWOMA: Look! We have won!

IGBOBA: Read their faces, my queen. Read the fear in their running feet.

(WARRIORS *are now before the king. They stand, distraught, and gasping.*)

IGBOBA: Break it, son. It's on a man's head that the cudgel is hit.

EBIE: It's not good, Your Majesty.

IGBOBA: I know. Break it, all the same.

EBIE: They swarmed us, My Lord ... like locusts on a tender maize farm. They overwhelmed us like an evil flood. We are finished-o, Your Majesty. Owa is finished.

IGBOBA: We granted the leper a handshake. Now he has engulfed us in his smelly embrace.

EBIE: As if that's not enough, they're on their way here.

IGBOBA, NWOMA: Here? To do what?

IGBOBA: (*Rushes to the palace shrine.*) Gods of our land!

EBIE: (*To his companions.*) He still believes in them!

(IGBOBA *continues his prayers in mime.* EBIE *makes to depart with his followers.*)

NWOMA: Chief Warrior, will you leave us unprotected?

EBIE: God forbid! All the warriors alive will be here before you blink twice. We will live or die with our king.

(*Exeunt* EBIE *and* WARRIORS. NWOMA *begins to fret and to wring her hand.*)

IGBOBA: (*Now audible.*) Arise and fight!

NWOMA: Yes-o. They had better.

IGBOBA: As they come, blind them.

NWOMA: Iseh!

IGBOBA: Cripple them.

NWOMA: Iseh!

IGBOBA: Confuse them.

NWOMA: Iseh!

IGBOBA: Or get ready for their fire. For it shall touch you before it reaches me.

NWOMA: My Lord, hurry! Let's run away!

IGBOBA: (*Facing her.*) Yes, run away. You and your son. Call me Nneka. You all must run away before the lepers come. They must not desecrate us further by laying their leprous fingers on our wives. They loot every good thing in every palace they conquer. You all should run away - with our carvings, if you can. You all, except my brother and the guards. We shall wait for them. And give them the last fight. Call everyone here.

NWOMA: Yes, My Lord.

(NWOMA *runs off. Blackout. "Imina" song swells up again, then fades. Slowly fade in Igboba's court.* IGBOBA, *now in war attire, is at the entrance, looking out. He is armed with a gun in his left hand and a spear in his right.* IWEKUBA, *also in war attire, rushes in with a gun and a spear.*)

IWEKUBA: They've broken through our defence again and will soon be here. They either arrest or kill, shooting dead even goats and sheep. They are burning houses. Owa is empty. Many escaped into the bush on their way to neighbouring villages – Ekome is one of them; many were killed in their flight; many, including my son and Acholem, have been arrested. And they're coming for you, My Lord.

IGBOBA: Let them come. I've been waiting for them. They'd find what they've been looking for ... Our warriors, led by your son, were they sleeping?

IWEKUBA: They did their best, My Lord. But it was like a few cockroaches confronting a large contingent of cocks.

(NNEKA, *in war attire, emerges from within, armed with a spear. At the same time,* NWOBI *and two guards emerge from a different door, all armed.*)

NNEKA: Let them come. Here they'll find cockroaches that swallow cocks and still yawn with hunger.

NWOBI: Yes, they will.

IGBOBA: (*to* NNEKA.) What are you still doing here? Didn't I order—

NNEKA: — me to run away and leave you alone here? Yes, you did, My Lord. But why should I do that? What life do I have left that I want to protect? Anxiety over you would kill me faster than the whiteman's gun. Since you refused to run away with us, wherever you are, there I'll be with you.

IGBOBA: Don't say I didn't warn you, my queen. It's the fly that didn't heed advice that followed the corpse into the grave.

NNEKA: God forbid that you become the corpse and I the heedless fly. White man! What can White man do to me, the daughter of the greatest hunter of this land and beyond? What can fire do to the feet of an iron pot? Have you forgotten that I hunted alongside my father and never missed my target? I that threw a spear and nailed a squirrel, a tiny little squirrel, to a palm tree! What can the white man do to me?

IGBOBA: You're old now, my queen.

NNEKA: But not older than you, My Lord. Yes, we are both old. But only a foolish ram will go dancing under the nose of a lion just because the lion is ill.

IWEKUBA: You're right, my Queen. The old lions here can still chew, swallow and digest the flesh and bones of the ram. They can still drink the blood of the ram like sweet palm wine.

NNEKA: That is why I'd have laughed My Lord to scorn if he opted to run away with his young wife. The idea really made me laugh: the great lion of Owa, running away from children! (*Brief laughter.*) Our future is in our past, My Lord. It's no longer available for us to protect. All we have left is our present. Let's fight the lepers together to protect our present.

IGBOBA: This is why I love you so much, my queen. Come. (*Hugs her closely without first dropping his weapons.*) You're a woman with the heart of a lion, always there to encourage me.

NNEKA: Thank you, My Lord.

IGBOBA: And we have more than our feeble present to fight for. We also have the future of Owa to fight for. The oracles may see a desolate land today, but Owa will have a future, a great future, and it is our duty to protect it.

IWEKUBA: If death comes from there, we die honourably.

NNEKA: That's right.

IGBOBA: But no one here will die.

ALL: Iseh!

IGBOBA: Those who come at us with death in their fingers will suck their own fingers.

ALL: Iseh!

IGBOBA: (*Makes to hand over his spear to* NNEKA.) Take this, my queen. It's been sharpened and poisoned by our ancestors.

NNEKA: Thank you, my lord.

(NNEKA *lays aside her spear, kneels, facing the entrance, arms stretched. All eyes are on her as* IGBOBA *approaches her ceremonially with the spear. Suddenly, she sees* LAWANI, *followed by* RUDKIN *and three soldiers, all armed, as they enter behind* IGBOBA *and* IWEKUBA. *The last soldier is also carrying handcuffs.* NNEKA *rises at once, jolting everyone.*)

NNEKA: (*Pointing.*) See!

(IGBOBA, *still holding the spear, and* IWEKUBA *turn at once.* NWOBI *and the guards hurtle forward.*)

IGBOBA: Stay back!

(*The guards move back, but* NWOBI *hesitates.*)

Stay back, my brother. Let us, the old ones, handle this. You might learn a thing or two from our methods. (*To* LAWANI.) You, again? How dare you set your feet again in my palace!

IWEKUBA: Are you deaf? The king orders you to disappear.

LAWANI: No one here can order me. There's only one king—

(*Like lightning,* IGBOBA, *using his astral body, spears* LAWANI *in the chest and he falls, groaning. A few moments after, blood begins to drip from Igboba's spear.*)

RUDKIN: Who did that?

IWEKUBA: Did what?

RUDKIN: Who struck him down, ape?

IWEKUBA: Your father is an ape!

RUDKIN: (*Noticing the blood on* IGBOBA's *spear.*) Oh, it's you! (*To soldiers.*) Disarm and arrest him, and the others too!

(*Soldiers move.*)

NNEKA: Don't move!

(*Soldiers stop and look back at* RUDKIN.)

RUDKIN: I command you—

(*As the first soldier moves further towards* IGBOBA, NNEKA *stretches out her right hand, draws the indigenous arsenal, uta mgba, from the air, and casts it at the soldier's flank. Only supernatural eyes see the sharp pebbles, pieces of irons and big needles as they stream from Nneka's hand into the soldier's flank. At once, the soldier screams and drops his gun as he grabs his flank with both hands. The two other soldiers exchange glances, then swiftly move to yank* LAWANI *off the ground, but he is dead. They drop him and take to their heels. The first soldier, still holding his flank, drags along after them.*)

RUDKIN: We'll be back. (*Follows his men.*)

IWEKUBA: Oyibo! Come and see war! Why are you running away so soon?

NWOBI: He's nothing without the blacks. Yet he brags!

IWEKUBA: (*Still to* RUDKIN.) Come and fight just one of us, the woman amongst us!

(*Simultaneously, all burst into laughter. Blackout. Marshal music rises in the background and is sustained for moments. Fade in slowly District Commissioner's Office, Agbor. There is a high table by the Eastern wall opposite the entrance. Behind it are two armed chairs. Some armed soldiers and police stand about. In front of the Northern wall, which is to the right of the high table,* GILPIN *is seated in his office chair by his office table.* IGBOBA, *in full royal regalia, is seated on a bench by a low table, facing* GILPIN. *Seated by his right is* NNEKA *and to the left,* NWOBI *and* IWEKUBA. *Two palace guards stand behind* IGBOBA, *one bearing his sceptre, the other gently fanning him. Enter* CHICHESTER *and* RUDKIN, *each followed by a fierce-looking orderly.* GILPIN *strikes his table with a gavel and everyone stands, the soldiers and police at attention. Only* IGBOBA *and* NNEKA *remain seated.* CHICHESTER *stands, facing* IGBOBA.)

SOLDIER 1: (*Hurtling forward, orders* IGBOBA.) Stand up!

CHICHESTER: Not necessary, Corporal.

SOLDIER I: (*Salutes.*) Yes, Sir!

CHICHESTER: And don't you ever again give orders in the presence of your superiors. Is that clear?

SOLDIER I: Yes, Sir!

CHICHESTER: (*To* IGBOBA.) How d'you do, my friend?

IGBOBA: I can't believe you're still calling me that.

CHICHESTER: Why? (*Sits on* GILPIN's *table.*)

IGBOBA: The rabbit does not look like one that was roasted by a friend for a friend. The meat is deliberately burnt beyond recognition.

CHICHESTER: I should say the same to you. But I'll use your other proverb, which I like very much: If you wake up in the morning and the chicken you've been rearing begins to chase you, run for your dear life, for your chicken might have grown teeth overnight. You grew teeth overnight, my friend, and that scared me to my bones.

IGBOBA: It wasn't me. It was Iredi who grew fangs and, like a mad hyena, started biting and killing my people.

CHICHESTER: Speak no ill of the dead.

IGBOBA: Well, you invited me to this meeting.

RUDKIN: Meeting?

SOLDIER 1: (*Jumping forward.*) Yes, Sir! Peace meeting, Sir!

(RUDKIN *looks questioningly at another soldier.*)

SOLDIER II: It was his idea, Sir.

SOLDIER 1: You ordered us to bring them by all means, Sir, and we brought them without violence and handcuffs.

IGBOBA: So, Mr DC, if it isn't for a peace meeting, what did you invite Igboba for?

CHICHESTER: Well, the meeting. Let's get on with it. (*Goes to take a seat by the high table, followed by RUDKIN. Their orderlies stand behind them. All those standing, except the soldiers and police, now sit.*)

CHICHESTER: (*To GILPIN.*) Read the charges.

GILPIN: He should be up standing, Sir.

CHICHESTER: Never mind.

GILPIN: Yes, Sir. (*Clears throat.*) That you, Head Chief Ektui Igboba —

IGBOBA: Mr DC—

CHICHESTER: You will be quiet and hear the charges against you, will you?

IGBOBA: Mr DC—

RUDKIN: He said, be quiet and listen!

IWEKUBA: Listen to what? How dare you order the Obi of Owa to be quiet?

NWOBI: Or are you now ready to fight? You that saw fight at the palace and took to your heels?

NNEKA: He couldn't even wait to fight me, a woman!

GILPIN: (*Striking his table with a gavel.*) Silence in court!

IGBOBA: So, Mr DC, this is really a court? So it was arrest that we were arrested?

NWOBI: I told you, my brother, that it was arrest that they came to arrest us, those tricksters, but because you heard the name of Chichester, you didn't believe me.

IGBOBA: I still won't believe till I hear it from Mr Chichester. (*To* CHICHESTER.) Mr Chichester, was it arrest you sent them to arrest us? The white man no longer has integrity? He now arrests Igboba with trickery? Invites him to a peace meeting and converts it to a trial?

RUDKIN: (*Impatiently.*) No one sent anyone to trick you. My orders to the soldiers were clear: "Go, disarm and arrest Igboba and everyone else in his palace and drag them to Agbor!"

IGBOBA: Disarm, arrest and drag! Sorry, they didn't do that. You sent the wrong people, Blacks with good home training. They know the story of Tortoise who declined to visit the lion who was ill. They know that the one who takes a message of abuse to the king is the one who abused him. So, they didn't act like the bastard, Lawani. (*Rises.*) Should you need your other stooges to re-run your errand — to go, disarm, arrest and drag Igboba and his household to your feet, we'll be waiting for them in our palace. (*Moves towards the entrance, followed by his people.*)

RUDKIN: Stop them!

(SOLDIER 2, *at the entrance, faces them but fires into the air. At once, he begins to scream.*)

SOLDIER 2: My hands! My hands are hanging!

(*Runs to* RUDKIN, *who, apparently, is scared and unable to help.*)

I can't bring my hands down! I can't drop my gun-o!

(*At once, every other Black armed soldier or police drops his gun and examines his hands.* CHICHESTER *rises, moves towards* IGBOBA.)

IWEKUBA: (*To* SOLDIER 2.) You like to scare royalty, don't you?

SOLDIER 2: I won't try it again, I swear. I won't try it again-o! (*Kneels, moving from* IGBOBA *to* IWEKUBA *and back.*) Please, help me! Please, cure my hand! It's getting so painful. Please, don't let me die!

CHICHESTER: Shut up!

SOLDIER 2: Yes, Sir, but my hands! Help me beg, Sir.

CHICHESTER: I said, shut up!

(SOLDIER 2 *now cringes without words.*)

CHICHESTER: (*To* IGBOBA.) My friend, I decided on this private trial in recognition of your exalted position as Head Chief. Your subjects, including your Prime Minister and your warriors, were tried and convicted in the open court and in the glare of commoners. They were sentenced to prison or exile or death.

IGBOBA: Who are those sentenced to death?

CHICHESTER: I don't have the list here. But all the ring leaders, especially those blood-thirsty warriors. They are at the government field, all chained up, constrained to witness the hanging of those condemned to death, before being led away. I didn't want you and your family to be treated likewise.

IGBOBA: So kind of you, my friend indeed! But take me to them.

CHICHESTER: Hear me out.

IGBOBA: (*Declaims.*) I said, take me to them!

CHICHESTER: (*To* IGBOBA.) Hear me out, please. You see, there are grave charges against you, including incitement of the peace-loving people of Owa against His Royal Majesty King Edward VII; ordering your warriors to kill Crewe-Read; and personally killing Sergeant Lawani. I want to save you, if I can. I want us to prove beyond reasonable doubt that you committed no such crimes. But, first, we have to enter your plea. Are you guilty or not guilty?

IGBOBA: I'm not a baby, Mr Chichester. I know the end of this trial. Be it private or public, I know the end. No matter my plea, guilty or not guilty, you'll banish me from my kingdom as you did Oba Ovonramwen of Benin, as you did King Nana of Itsekiri land. Listen, if my people deserve to die by hanging because they dared to defend their fatherland against oppressive aggression from you and your people, I desire to die with them because they ran my errand. Take me to them. If I must live, even in exile, my people must live also. Exile will end one day, whether you like it or not, and I'll need my subjects, for what is a king without subjects? Owa will need them, for what is a kingdom without people? I can assure you that your evil grip on Owa will not last forever. The evil bottom of King Edward will not spread over the throne of my ancestors forever. (*To* IWEKUBA.) Release this fool.

CHICHESTER: Thank you.

IWEKUBA: (*Slaps* SOLDIER 2 *on the back.*) Put your hands down, fool.

(SOLDIER 2 *lowers his hands, drops his gun and prostrates before* IGBOBA.)

IGBOBA: I go to my people. (*Moves, but stops again.*) Mr DC, how can you prove beyond reasonable doubt who struck this fool? (*Pause.*) That was how Lawani was killed and you've just charged me with killing him. Did anyone truly see *me* strike him? Captain Rudkin came with him and he's here now. Ask him, did he see me strike Lawani? But when it comes to dealing with Blacks, the white man always gives the verdict before finding the proof. Take me to my people.

(IGBOBA *strides off, followed by his entourage. Slow fade-out as* CHICHESTER *turns round to confer with* RUDKIN *in whispers. In the darkness that follows, Imina song, sung sorrowfully, pervades the air. As twilight descends, a line of prisoners in chains is crossing the arena, almost in silhouette, escorted by inscrutable but well-armed soldiers. As they move languidly, their chains clang to the beat of the song. At the rear are a few who are not chained:* NNEKA, IGBOBA, ACHOLEM *and* IWEKUBA. *Suddenly,* NWOBI, *apparently the last man in chains, speaks.*)

NWOBI: We are the cripple in a desolate land
　　　The desolate land soaked with blood of its children
　　　Blood spilled by the nuzzles of the lepers' guns
　　　Lepers' guns that kill their hosts
　　　Or hang them in the gallows
　　　Or cripple them with chains
　　　And desolate their land
　　　Yes, we are
　　　The cripple in a desolate land.

ACHOLEM: May I remind us
　　　That the other oracle said, Salute your king
　　　Isn't he worth the salutation?
　　　He saved us from the noose
　　　Are we less guilty than those they had hanged?
　　　He offered his neck
　　　He offered his neck
　　　The white man declined to hang him
　　　Because of what the world would say
　　　The Obi declined to walk without his people
　　　Because of what his conscience would say
　　　Because of what his ancestors would say
　　　Because Obi Agun is a man with a man's heart
　　　Didn't Ekome run away?
　　　Obi Agun, we salute you!

IWEKUBA: The whiteman's gun is a mere stick
　　　To Obi Agun, his queen and me

96

The body of the goat does not bear whip marks
Yet the Obi keeps us in this line of prisoners
For the love of our land
The whiteman's gun is a mere stick
To my son and to many warriors of Owa
Yet the whiteman's noose cut
The necks of their lives
For the love of our land.

IGBOBA: Wait, my people, wait
A man does not pass by his compound
Without marking it with his foot
Neither the whiteman's chains
On our legs
Nor the whiteman's guns
At our backs
By our sides
At our front
Can stop our feet
From marking our compound
As a sign that we shall return.

(*Everyone stops, slowly backs the audience and draws a right footmark towards Owa. They turn again and move on. As the line disappears completely, lights come on the narrators.*)

NARRATOR I: Who dipped his hand in the pot of the dead?

NARRATOR II: Can he free his hand? Or would the pot be broken first? Who would break the pot of the dead?

MOA/AUDIENCE: Tell us!

NARRATOR II: We will, but that will be in the next era. This is the end of this era. To get the answers to those questions, you must remain alive till the next era. Will you?

MOA/AUDIENCE: Yes, we will!

NARRATOR I, NARRATOR II: See you then.

(NARRATOR I *and* NARRATOR II *bow deeply as* "Imina" *wells up to a crescendo and fades off.*)

THE END

Kraftgriots

Also in the series (DRAMA) *(continued)*

Sam Ukala: *Two Plays* (2008)
Ahmed Yerima: *Akuabata* (2008)
Kayode Animasaun: *Sand-eating Dog* (2008)
Ahmed Yerima: *Tuti* (2008)
Ahmed Yerima: *Mojagbe* (2009)
Ahmed Yerima: *The Ife Quartet* (2009)
Peter Omoko: *Battles of Pleasure* (2009)
'Muyiwa Ojo: *Memoirs of a Lunatic* (2009)
John Iwuh: *Spellbound* (2009)
Osita C. Ezenwanebe: *Dawn of Full Moon* (2009)
Ahmed Yerima: *Dami's Cross & Atika's Well* (2009)
Osita C. Ezenwanebe: *Giddy Festival* (2009)
Ahmed Yerima: *Little Drops ...* (2009)
Arnold Udoka: *Long Walk to a Dream* (2009), winner, 2010 ANA/NDDC J.P. Clark
    drama prize
Arnold Udoka: *Inyene: A Dance Drama* (2009)
Chris Anyokwu: *Termites* (2010)
Julie Okoh: *A Haunting Past* (2010)
Arnold Udoka: *Mbarra: A Dance Drama* (2010)
Chukwuma Anyanwu: *Another Weekend, Gone!* (2010)
Oluseyi Adigun: *Omo Humuani: Abubaka Olusola Saraki, Royal Knight of Kwara*
    (2010)
Eni Jologho Umuko: *The Scent of Crude Oil* (2010)
Olu Obafemi: *Ogidi Mandate* (2010), winner, 2011 ANA/NDDC J.P. Clark drama
    prize
Ahmed Yerima: *Ajagunmale* (2010)
Ben Binebai: *Drums of the Delta* (2010)
'Diran Ademiju-Bepo: *Rape of the Last Sultan* (2010)
Chris Iyimoga: *Son of a Chief* (2010)
Arnold Udoka: *Rainbow Over the Niger & Nigeriana* (2010)
Julie Okoh: *Our Wife Forever* (2010)
Barclays Ayakoroma: *A Matter of Honour* (2010)
Barclays Ayakoroma: *Dance on His Grave* (2010)
Isiaka Aliagan: *Olubu* (2010)
Emmanuel Emasealu: *Nerves* (2011)
Osita Ezenwanebe: *Adaugo* (2011)
Osita Ezenwanebe: *Daring Destiny* (2011)
Ahmed Yerima: *No Pennies for Mama* (2011)
Ahmed Yerima: *Mu'adhin's Call* (2011)
Barclays Ayakoroma: *A Chance to Survive and Other Plays* (2011)
Barclays Ayakoroma: *Castles in the Air* (2011)
Arnold Udoka: *Akon* (2011)
Arnold Udoka: *Still Another Night* (2011)
Sunnie Ododo: *Hard Choice* (2011)
Sam Ukala: *Akpakaland and Other Plays* (2011)
Greg Mbajiorgu: *Wake Up Everyone!* (2011)

Ahmed Yerima: *Three Plays* (2011)
Ahmed Yerima: *Igatibi* (2012)
Esanmabeke Opuofeni: *Song of the Gods* (2012)
Karo Okokoh: *Teardrops of the Gods* (2012)
Esanmabeke Opuofeni: *The Burning House* (2012)
Dan Omatsola: *Olukume* (2012)
Alex Roy-Omoni: *Morontonu* (2012)
Chinyere G. Okafor: *New Toyi-Toyi* (2012)
Greg Mbajiorgu: *The Prime Minister's Son* (2012)
Karo Okokoh: *Sunset So Soon* (2012)
Sunnie Ododo: *Two Liberetti: To Return from the Void & Vanishing Vapour* (2012)
Gabriel B. Egbe: *Emani* (2012)
Shehu Sani: *When Clerics Kill* (2013)
Ahmed Yerima: *Tafida & Other Plays* (2013)
Osita Ezenwanebe: *Shadows on Arrival* (2013)
Praise C. Daniel-Inim: *Married But Single and Other plays* (2013)
Bosede Ademilua-Afolayan: *Look Back in Gratitude* (2013)
Greg Mbajiorgu: *Beyond the Golden Prize* (2013)
Ahmed Yerima: *Heart of Stone* (2013)
Julie Umukoro: *Marriage Coup* (2013)
Praise C. Daniel-Inim: *Deacon Dick* (2013)
Wale Odebade: *Ariwowanye (The Uneasy Head)* (2013)
Soji Cole: *Maybe Tomorrow* (2013)
Wumi Raji: *Another Life* (2013)